SANSKRIT PROVERBS
SANSKRIT LOKOKTULU TRILINGUAL

SANSKRIT PROVERBS
SANSKRIT LOKOKTULU TRILINGUAL

Printed in the Devanagri and Telegu Characters

M. W. Carr

GYAN

Published by

Gyan Publishing House
5, Ansari Road
Daryaganj, New Delhi-110002
Phone: 011-47034999, 9811692060
E-mail: books@gyanbooks.com

Distribution Network
gyanbooks.com
India, USA, Canada, UK, Australia, France

ISBN : 978-81-212-3983-7 (PB)
First Published, Madras, 1868

2nd Impression 2020

Printed at: Gyan Press, Delhi.

సంస్కృతలోకోక్తులు.

SANSCRIT PROVERBS.

अ.

1. अंगारश्शतधौतेन मलिनत्वं न मुंचति ॥

అంగారశ్శతధౌతేన మలినత్వం న ముంచతి॥

The blackness cannot be removed from charcoal by a hundred washings.

स्वभावो यादृशो यस्य न जहाति कदाचन।
अंगारश्शतधौतेन मलिनत्वं न मुंचति ॥ इतिचाणक्यधृतं ॥

స్వభావో యాదృశో యస్య న జహాతి కదాచన।
అంగారశ్శతధౌతేన మలినత్వం న ముంచతి॥ ఇతిచాణక్యధృతం॥

Whatever one's nature be, it never changes; the blackness is not removed from charcoal by a hundred washings. (Kavitâratnâkara 161).

" Can the Ethiopian change his skin or the leopard his spots ?"
Jeremiah xiii. 23.

2. अंततोऽश्मापि जीर्यति ॥

అంతతోఽశ్మాపి జీర్యతి॥

The stone is worn away at last.

3. अंतस्तापो बहिश्शीतं ॥

అంతస్తాపో బహిశ్శీతం॥

Inward heat, outward coolness.

(See TELUGU No. 4, &c.—also No. 2022.)

Outward friendship, inward hate.

4. अंधस्य दीपो बधिरस्य गीतं मूर्खस्य शास्त्रं किमु सानुरागं ॥
అంధస్య దీపో బధిరస్య గీతం మూర్ఖస్య శాస్త్రం కిము సానురాగం॥

Is a lamp pleasing to the blind, a song to the deaf, or science to the fool ?

5. अग्निनाग्निस्समिध्यते ॥
అగ్నినాగ్నిస్సమిధ్యతే॥

With fire, fire is kindled.

Like produces like.

अग्निनाग्निः समिध्यते कविर्गृहपतिर्युवा। हव्यवाड् जुह्वास्यः ॥
అగ్నినాగ్నిః సమిధ్యతే కవిర్గృహపతిర్యువా। హవ్యవాడ్ జుహ్వాస్యః॥

"AGNI, the ever young and wise, the guardian of the dwelling (of the sacrificer), the bearer of offerings, whose mouth is (the vehicle) of oblations is kindled by AGNI." (Ṛig-veda-saṁhitâ 12, 6.—Wilson's trans.)*

6. अग्निर्वैद्यमतःपरं ॥
అగ్నిర్వైద్యమతఃపరం॥

Hereafter treatment by fire.

An ambiguous phrase used by a physician : it may either refer to cauterization of the affected part, or to cremation of the whole body.

7. अजायुद्धे ऋषिश्राद्धे प्रभाते मेघडंबरे।
दंपत्योः कलहे चैव बह्वारंभो लघुक्रिया ॥
అజాయుద్ధే ఋషిశ్రాద్ధే ప్రభాతే మేఘడంబరే।
దంపత్యోః కలహే చైవ బహ్వారంభో లఘుక్రియా॥

In the fighting of she-goats, in a Ṛishi's obsequial rites, in the gathering of clouds at the dawn, in the squabbles of husband and wife, the beginning is great, and the doings are small.

* "That is, the *Âhavanīya* fire, into which the oblation is poured, is lighted by the application of other fire whether taken from the household fire or produced by attrition." (Wilson's note.)

8. अति सर्वत्र वर्जयेत् ॥
అతి సర్వత్ర వర్జయేత్ ॥

Excess is to be avoided in all things.

अतिदानाद्धतः कर्णस्त्वतिलोभात्सुयोधनः ।
अतिकामाद्दशग्रीवस्त्वति सर्वत्र वर्जयेत् ॥
అతిదానాద్ధతః కర్ణస్త్వతిలోభాత్సుయోధనః।
అతికామాద్దశగ్రీవస్త్వతి సర్వత్ర వర్జయేత్॥

Karṇa was ruined by excessive liberality, Suyodhana by excessive avarice, Daśagrîva by excessive lust—Excess is to be avoided in all things.

9. अति सर्वत्र गर्ह्यते ॥
అతి సర్వత్ర గర్హ్యతే॥

Excess is blamed in all things.

10. अतिस्नेहः पापाशंकी ॥
అతిస్నేహః పాపాశంకీ॥

Excessive friendship [causes] doubt of sin.

11. अत्युच्छ्रायः पतनहेतुः ॥
అత్యుచ్ఛ్రాయః పతనహేతుః॥

Too great exaltation is the cause of a downfall.

(See TELUGU No. 1531.)

12. अदानदोषेण भवेद्दरिद्रो दारिद्र्यदोषेण करोति पापं ।
पापादवश्यं नरकं प्रयाति पुनर्दरिद्रः पुनरेव पापी ॥
అదానదోషేణ భవేద్దరిద్రో దారిద్ర్యదోషేణ కరోతి పాపం।
పాపాదవశ్యం నరకం ప్రయాతి పునర్దరిద్రః పునరేవ పాపీ॥

By the crime of not giving alms, [a man] becomes poor; by the defect of poverty, he commits sin; by sin he certainly goes to hell; again [he becomes] poor, again [he becomes] a sinner.

13. अदृष्टपादपे देशे एरंडोपि द्रुमायते ॥
అదృష్టపాదపే దేశే ఏరండోపి ద్రుమాయతే॥

In the country where no tree is seen, even the castor oil plant is called a tree.

यत्र विद्वज्जनो नास्ति श्लाघ्यस्तत्राल्पधीरपि ।
निरस्तपादपे देशे एरंडोपि द्रुमायते ॥
యత్ర విద్వజ్జనో నాస్తి శ్లాఘ్యస్తత్రాల్పధీరపి।
నిరస్తపాదపే దేశే ఏరండోపి ద్రుమాయతే॥

Where there is no learned man, there even one of little intellect is to be praised; in a place without trees, even the castor-oil plant is considered a tree.—Hitopadeśa, Book I.

14. अद्य भक्ष्यो धनुर्गुणः ॥
అద్య భక్ష్యో ధనుర్గుణః॥

To-day the bow string is to be eaten.

Referring to the story of the parsimonious jackal in the Hitopadeśa, Book I.

15. अद्य युद्धं त्वया मया ॥
అద్య యుద్ధం త్వయా మయా॥

Now a combat between thee and me!

सप्तसिंहा जिताः पूर्वं पंचव्याघ्रास्त्रयोगजाः ।
पश्यंतु देवतास्सर्वा अद्य युद्धं त्वया मया ॥ इतीतिहासः ॥
సప్తసింహాః జితాః పూర్వం పంచవ్యాఘ్రాస్త్రయోగజాః।
పశ్యంతు దేవతాస్సర్వా అద్య యుద్ధం త్వయా మయా॥ ఇతీతిహాసః॥

Seven lions, five tigers, and three elephants have ere this been conquered by me; to-day a combat between thee and me, let all the gods behold it! (Kavitâratnâkara 17.)

16. अधमा सेवकावृत्तिः ॥
అధమా సేవకావృత్తిః॥

Servitude is the lowest occupation.

17. **अधिकस्याधिकं फलं ॥**

అధికస్యాధికం ఫలం॥

More is the fruit of much.

18. **अनभ्यासे विषं शास्त्रमजीर्णे भोजनं विषं ॥**

అనభ్యాసే విషం శాస్త్రమజీర్ణే భోజనం విషం॥

Want of practice [makes] science poison, indigestion [makes] food poison.

(cf. Böhtlingk's *Indische Sprüche*, I. 87).

A little knowledge is a dangerous thing.

Practise not your art, and 'twill soon depart. (German.)*

19. **अनाथप्रेतसंस्कारात्कोटियज्ञफलं लभेत् ॥**

అనాథప్రేతసంస్కారాత్కోటియజ్ఞఫలం లభేత్॥

By performing the obsequies of an unclaimed corpse, the reward of ten million sacrifices will be obtained.

20. **अनाथो देवरक्षकः ॥**

అనాథో దేవరక్షకః॥

The destitute has God for his protector.

(See TELUGU No. 1160.)

" Thou art a God of the afflicted, an helper of the oppressed, an upholder of the weak, a protector of the forlorn, a Saviour of them that are without hope." Judith ix. 11.

21. **अनामिका सार्थवती बभूव ॥**

అనామికా సార్థవతీ బభూవ॥

The nameless has become possessed of a meaning.

Anâmikâ (" having no name") is the ring finger.

---

* Wer die kunst nicht übt, verlernt sie bald.

पुरा कवीनां गणनाप्रसंगे कनिष्ठिकाधिष्ठितकालिदासा।
अद्यापि तत्तुल्यकवेरभावादनामिका सार्थवती बभूव॥
పురా కవీనాం గణనాప్రసంగే కనిష్ఠికాధిష్ఠితకాళిదాసా।
అద్యాపి తత్తుల్యకవేరభావాదనామికా సార్థవతీ బభూవ॥

Formerly on an occasion of numbering the poets, Kâlidâsa having been placed on the little finger (i. e. first) and no poet equal to him having up to this time existed, the nameless (ring finger) has become possessed of a meaning.

(cf. Böhtlingk's *Indische Sprüche*, 2. 1798).

22. अनायका विनश्यंति नश्यंति शिशुनायकाः।
स्त्रीनायका विनश्यंति नश्यंति बहुनायकाः॥
అనాయకా వినశ్యంతి నశ్యంతి శిశునాయకాః।
స్త్రీనాయకా వినశ్యంతి నశ్యంతి బహునాయకాః॥

Those without a leader perish; those with a youthful leader perish; those with a female leader perish; those with many leaders perish.

23. अनाश्वासितदुःखिते मनसि सर्वमसह्यं॥
అనాశ్వాసితదుఃఖితే మనసి సర్వమసహ్యం॥

When the mind is grieved and unconsoled, all is disgust.

24. अनित्यानि शरीराणि विभवोनैव शाश्वतः।
नित्यं सन्निहितो मृत्युः कर्तव्यो धर्मसंग्रहः॥
అనిత్యాని శరీరాణి విభవోనైవ శాశ్వతః।
నిత్యం సన్నిహితో మృత్యుః కర్తవ్యో ధర్మసంగ్రహః॥

Bodies are transitory; riches are not lasting; death is always at hand; [therefore] virtue should be practised.

25. अन्नदातस्सुखी भव ॥

అన్నదాతస్సుఖీ భవ॥

O giver of food! be happy.

A phrase used in returning thanks.

26. अन्नमूलं बलं पुंसां ॥

అన్నమూలం బలం పుంసాం॥

The strength of men is rooted in food.

अन्नमूलं बलंपुंसां बलमूलंहि जीवनं ।
तस्माद्यत्नेन संरक्षेत्बलंच कुशलो भिषक् ॥
అన్నమూలం బలంపుంసాం బలమూలంహి జీవనం।
తస్మాద్యత్నేన సంరక్షేత్ బలంచ కుశలో భిషక్॥

The strength of man is rooted in food, the life is rooted in strength; therefore the skilful physician should carefully preserve the strength. (Kavitâratnâkara 201.)

27. अन्नस्य क्षुधितं पात्रं ॥

అన్నస్య క్షుధితం పాత్రం॥

The hungered is worthy of food.

28. अन्नानुरूपास्तनुरूपबुद्धयः ॥

అన్నానురూపాస్తనురూపబుద్ధయః॥

The body, form, and sense depend upon the food.

29. अन्यथा चिंतितं कार्यं दैवमन्यत्र चिंतयेत् ॥

అన్యథా చింతితం కార్యం దైవమన్యత్ర చింతయేత్॥

A plan considered [by man] in one way is considered by God in another.

(See TELUGU No. 1056.)

Human counsels are directed from heaven. (Latin.)*

* Humana consilia divinitus gubernantur.

30. अपृष्टोपि शुभं ब्रूयात् ॥
అపృష్టోపి శుభం బ్రూయాత్॥

Although unasked, you should speak auspiciously.

31. अबद्धंवा सुबद्धंवा कुंतीपुत्रो विनायकः ॥
అబద్ధంవా సుబద్ధంవా కుంతీపుత్రో వినాయకః॥

Be it truth, or be it falsehood, Vinâyaka was the son of Kuntî.

32. अभावे विरक्तिः ॥
అభావే విరక్తిః॥

In not having is disgust.

Disgust is simulated with regard to that which is unattainable.

अभावे विरक्तिरसंभावितानां मंत्रावृत्तिर्दरिद्रस्य देवताभक्तिः ॥
అభావే విరక్తిరసంభావితానాం మంత్రావృత్తిర్దరిద్రస్య దేవతాభక్తిః॥

In the non-existence is disgust ; there is repetition of Mantras by those who are unhonored ; there is trust in God by the poor.

33. अभ्यासानुसरी विद्या बुद्धिः कर्मानुसारिणी ।
उद्योगानुसरी लक्ष्मीः फलं भाग्यानुसारिच ॥
అభ్యాసానుసరీ విద్యా బుద్ధిః కర్మానుసారిణీ।
ఉద్యోగానుసరీ లక్ష్మీః ఫలం భాగ్యానుసారిచ॥

Learning depends on practice, intellect on former deeds ; wealth follows exertion, and success, good fortune.

34. अयं पटाटोपः कौपीनसंरक्षणार्थः ॥
అయం పటాటోపః కౌపీనసంరక్షణార్థః॥

This pomp is for the protection of the clout.

Said by a Sannyâsî when asked why his style of living was inconsistent with his profession. To protect his rags from the rats he got a cat, to get milk for the cat he bought a cow, to tend the cow he hired a servant, and for his servant he procured a wife.

35. अरसिकजनसंभाषणतोरसिकजनेन वरं वाक्कलहः ॥

అరసికజనసంభాషణతోరసికజనేన వరం వాక్కలహః॥

To quarrel with a man of good speech is better than to converse with a man of rude address.

36. अर्थस्य पुरुषो दासः ॥

అర్థస్య పురుషో దాసః॥

Man is the slave of money.

अर्थस्य पुरुषो दासो दासस्त्वर्थो न कस्यचित् ।
इति सत्यं महाराज बद्धस्त्वार्थेच कौरवैः ॥

అర్థస్య పురుషో దాసో దాసస్త్వర్థో న కస్యచిత్।
ఇతి సత్యం మహారాజ బద్ధస్త్వార్థేచ కౌరవైః॥

Man is the slave of money, money is the slave of no one ; this is true O Mahârâja! By money I have been made subject to the Kauravas.

(cf. Böhtlingk's *Indische Sprüche* 1. 214).

37. अर्था गृहे निवर्तंते श्मशाने मित्रबांधवाः ।
सुकृतं दुष्कृतंचैव गच्छंतमनुगच्छति ॥

అర్థా గృహే నివర్తంతే శ్మశానే మిత్రబాంధవాః।
సుకృతం దుష్కృతంచైవ గచ్ఛంతమనుగచ్ఛతి॥

Wealth stops at the house, friends and relatives at the grave ; good deeds and evil deeds follow the dying man.

38. अर्थातुराणां न गुरुर्नबंधुः कामातुराणां न भयं न लज्जा ।
विद्यातुराणां न सुखं न निद्रा क्षुधातुराणां न रुचिर्नपक्वं ॥

అర్థాతురాణాం న గురుర్నబంధుః కామాతురాణాం న భయం న లజ్జా।
విద్యాతురాణాం న సుఖం న నిద్రా, క్షుధాతురాణాం న రుచిర్నపక్వం॥

Those eager to amass wealth regard neither priests nor relations ; those eager to indulge lust feel neither fear nor shame ; those eager in the pursuit of knowledge care not for comfort or sleep ; those eager to satisfy hunger regard neither the flavour nor the cookery.

(cf. Böhtlingk's *Indische Sprüche* 3. 5597.)

39. अर्थानामार्जने दुःखमार्जितानांच रक्षणे ।
नाशे दुःखं व्यये दुःखं किमर्थं दुःखभाजनं ॥

అర్థానామార్జనే దుఃఖమార్జితానాంచ రక్షణే।
నాశే దుఃఖం వ్యయే దుఃఖం కిమర్థం దుఃఖభాజనం॥

There is pain in acquiring wealth, pain in preserving what has been acquired, pain in its loss, and pain in its expenditure—why have such a receptacle of sorrow ?

40. अर्थेन सर्वे वशाः ॥

అర్థేన సర్వే వశాః॥

All are made subject by money.

माता निंदति नाभिनंदति पिता भ्राता न संभाषते ।
भृत्यः कुप्यति नानुगच्छति सुतः कांताच नालिंगते ।
अर्थप्रार्थनशंकया न कुरुतेप्यालापमात्रं सुहृत् ।
तस्मादर्थमुपार्जयश्शृणुसखे चार्थेन सर्वे वशाः ॥

మాతా నిందతి నాభి నందతి పితా భ్రాతా న సంభాషతే।
భృత్యః కుప్యతి నానుగచ్ఛతి సుతః కాంతాచ నాలింగతే।
అర్థప్రార్థన శంకయానకురుతే ప్యాలాపమాత్రం సుహృత్।
తస్మాదర్థముపార్జయశ్శృణుసఖే చార్థేన సర్వే వశాః॥

The mother rails, the father is displeased, the brother speaks not, the servant sulks, the son accompanies not, the wife embraces not, and for fear of being asked for money even the friend addresses not—listen therefore O friend ! Acquire wealth, for all are made subject by money. (Kavitâratnâkara 20.)

41. अल्पविद्यो महागर्वः ॥

అల్పవిద్యో మహాగర్వః॥

Little learning, much pride.

(See TELUGU No. 454, &c.)

42. **अल्पारंभः क्षेमकरः ॥**

అల్పారంభః క్షేమకరః॥

A small beginning is good.

To attempt too much at first is unwise.

Every beginning is feeble. (Latin.)*

43. **अवश्यं पितुराचारः ॥**

అవశ్యం పితురాచారః॥

A father's rule is binding [on the son.]

Âchâra is "an established rule of conduct." (Wilson.)

44. **अवश्यमेव भोक्तव्यं कृतं कर्म शुभाशुभं ॥**

అవశ్యమేవ భోక్తవ్యం కృతం కర్మ శుభాశుభం॥

[The reward of] deeds done, be they good or evil, will assuredly be received.

मा भुक्तं क्षीयते कर्म कल्पकोटिशतैरपि ।
अवश्यमेव भोक्तव्यं कृतं कर्म शुभाशुभं ॥

మా భుక్తం క్షీయతే కర్మ కల్పకోటిశతైరపి।
అవశ్యమేవ భోక్తవ్యం కృతం కర్మ శుభాశుభం॥

The result of [evil] deeds, unsuffered, decays not even by hundreds of crores of Kalpas.

45. **अवस्था पूज्यते राजन्नशरीरं शरीरिणां ॥**

అవస్థా పూజ్యతే రాజన్నశరీరం శరీరిణాం॥

O king! the position, not the body of corporeal beings is worshipped.

अवस्था पूज्यते राजन्नशरीरं शरीरिणां ।
तदा वनचरो राम इदानीं नृपतां गतः ॥

అవస్థా పూజ్యతే రాజన్నశరీరం శరీరిణాం।
తదా వనచరో రామ ఇదానీం నృపతాం గతః॥

O King! the position—not the body—of corporeal beings is worshipped; Râma who once was a wanderer in the forests has now obtained kinghood. (Kavitâratnâkara 140.)

---

* Omne principium est debile.

46. अविचारपुरीमध्ये यः पलायति जीवति ॥
అవిచారపురీమధ్యే యః పలాయతి జీవతి॥
He who flees from an ill-governed town will live.

47. अव्यवस्थितचित्तस्य प्रसादोपि भयंकरः ॥
అవ్యవస్థితచిత్తస్య ప్రసాదోపి భయంకరః॥
Even the favor of a man of ill-regulated mind is to be dreaded.

क्वचिद्रुष्टः क्वचित्तुष्टो रुष्टस्तुष्टः क्षणेक्षणे ।
अव्यवस्थितचित्तस्य प्रसादोपि भयंकरः ॥
క్వచిద్రుష్టః క్వచిత్తుష్టో రుష్టస్తుష్టః క్షణేక్షణే।
అవ్యవస్థితచిత్తస్య ప్రసాదోపి భయంకరః॥

Sometimes angry, sometimes pleased, angry one moment and pleased another; even the favor of a man of ill-regulated mind is to be dreaded.

48. असंतुष्टो द्विजो नष्टस्संतुष्ट इव पार्थिवः ॥
అసంతుష్టో ద్విజో నష్టస్సంతుష్ట ఇవ పార్థివః॥
A discontented Brahman is lost [to the world] like a contented king.

49. असतां धर्मबुद्धिश्चेत्सतां संतापकारणं ॥
అసతాం ధర్మబుద్ధిశ్చేత్సతాం సంతాపకారణం॥
If bad men become charitable, it will be a cause of grief to the good.

50. असह्यं ज्ञातिदुर्वाक्यं ॥
అసహ్యం జ్ఞాతిదుర్వాక్యం॥
An evil word from a cousin is insufferable.

वरं रामशरस्सह्यो न च वैभीषणं वचः ।
असह्यं ज्ञातिदुर्वाक्यं मेघांतरितरौद्रवत् ॥
వరం రామశరస్సహ్యో న చ వైభీషణం వచః।
అసహ్యం జ్ఞాతిదుర్వాక్యం మేఘాంతరితరౌద్రవత్॥

Râma's dart is easier to bear than Vibhîshaṇa's word; an evil word from a cousin is insufferable, like the fury in the clouds.

51. असारे खलु संसारे सारं श्वशुरमंदिरं ॥

అసారే ఖలు సంసారే సారం శ్వశురమందిరం॥

Worldly pursuits are surely unprofitable, but there is something to be had in the father-in-law's house.

असारे खलु संसारे सारं श्वशुरमंदिरं ।
हिमालये हरश्शेते हरिश्शेते महोदधौ ॥

అసారే ఖలు సంసారే సారం శ్వశురమందిరం।
హిమాలయే హరశ్శేతే హరిశ్శేతే మహోదధౌ॥

There is truly nothing profitable in the world, the father-in-law's house is best; Śiva sleeps on the Himâlayas (father of Durgâ) and Vishṇu sleeps on the great ocean (father of Lakshmî). (cf. Böhtlingk 1. 290.)

52 अहिंसा परमो धर्मः ॥

అహింసా పరమో ధర్మః॥

Non-injury is the highest duty.

(cf. Hitopadeśa Book I. and Böhtlingk's *Indische Sprüche* 1. 301.)

आ.

53. आकारो ह्रस्वः गुणास्तु विपुलाः॥

ఆకారో హ్రస్వః గుణాస్తు విపులాః॥

The form is small, the qualities are great.

A little body often harbours a great soul.

54. आचारः प्रथमो धर्मः ॥

ఆచారః ప్రథమో ధర్మః॥

The observance of ordinances is the first duty.

55. आजगाम यदा लक्ष्मीर्नारिकेलफलांबुवत् ।
निर्जगाम यदा लक्ष्मीर्गजभुक्तकपित्थवत् ॥ इतिनीतिशास्त्रं ॥

ఆజగామ యదా లక్ష్మీర్నారికేలఫలాంబువత్।
నిర్జగామ యదా లక్ష్మీర్గజభుక్తకపిత్థవత్॥

When the goddess of wealth came, it was like the water in a cocoanut; when she departed it was like the wood-apple eaten by an elephant.

(See TELUGU No. 445.)

56. आतुरे नियमो नास्ति ॥

ఆతురే నియమో నాస్తి॥

For the sick man, there is no rule.

He is exempted from the observance of the ceremonial law.

57. आत्मच्छिद्रं न जानंति परच्छिद्रानुसारिणः ॥

ఆత్మచ్ఛిద్రం న జానంతి పరచ్ఛిద్రానుసారిణః॥

They know not their own defects who search for the defects of others.

58. स्त्रीबुद्धिः प्रलयंकरी ॥

స్త్రీబుద్ధిః ప్రలయంకరీ॥

Woman's counsel is destructive.

आत्मबुद्धिस्सुखंचैव गुरुबुद्धिर्विशेषतः ।
परबुद्धिर्विनाशाय स्त्रीबुद्धिः प्रलयंकरी ॥

ఆత్మబుద్ధిస్సుఖంచైవ గురుబుద్ధిర్విశేషతః।
పరబుద్ధిర్వినాశాయ స్త్రీబుద్ధిః ప్రలయంకరీ॥

One's own resolve is happy, the priest's advice is better; another's advice is for one's ruin, woman's counsel is destructive.

59. आत्मवत्सर्वभूतानि यः पश्यति स पश्यति ॥
ఆత్మవత్సర్వభూతాని యః పశ్యతి స పశ్యతి॥

He who looks upon all living beings as upon himself, sees.

मातृवत्परदारांश्च परद्रव्याणि लोष्टवत् ।
आत्मवत्सर्वभूतानि यः पश्यति स पश्यति॥
మాతృవత్పరదారాంశ్చ పరద్రవ్యాణి లోష్టవత్।
ఆత్మవత్సర్వభూతాని యః పశ్యతి స పశ్యతి॥

He who looks upon other men's wives as his mother, and other men's money as clods of earth, he who considers all creatures as himself—he sees [with spiritual wisdom].

(cf. Böhtlingk's *Indische Sprüche*, 2. 2173).

Do as you would be done by.

60. आत्मवन्मन्यते जगत् ॥
ఆత్మవన్మన్యతే జగత్॥

[Every man] thinks the world like himself.

61. आत्मशक्तिसमं कोपं यो जानाति स पंडितः ॥
ఆత్మశక్తిసమం కోపం యో జానాతి స పండితః॥

He is wise whose wrath is limited by his power.

If you cannot bite, never shew your teeth.

62. आत्मानं सततं रक्षेत् ॥
ఆత్మానం సతతం రక్షేత్॥

You should always save yourself.

आपदर्थं धनं रक्षेद्दारान्रक्षेद्धनैरपि ।
आत्मानं सततं रक्षेद्दारैरपि धनैरपि ॥
ఆపదర్థం ధనం రక్షేద్దారాన్రక్షేద్ధనైరపి।
ఆత్మానం సతతం రక్షేద్దారైరపి ధనైరపి॥

You should save money for [a time of] distress, you should save your wife even with [the expenditure of] money; you should always save yourself even with [the sacrifice of] wife and money.

Self is the first object of charity. (Latin.)*

* Prima sibi charitas.

63. आपदर्थे धनं रक्षेत् ॥
ఆపదర్థే ధనం రక్షేత్॥
Money should be saved for a time of need.

आपदर्थे धनं रक्षेत् श्रीमतामापदः कुतः ।
सा चेदपगता लक्ष्मीस्संचितार्थो विनश्यति ॥
ఆపదర్థే ధనం రక్షేత్ శ్రీమతామాపదః కుతః।
సా చేదపగతా లక్ష్మీస్సంచితార్థో వినశ్యతి॥

Money should be saved for a time of need, how can distress reach the rich? If fortune depart, the wealth acquired will be lost.

64. आयुरन्नं प्रयच्छति ॥
ఆయురన్నం ప్రయచ్ఛతి॥
Duration of life gives food.

i. e. So long as a man is destined to live, food will not be wanting.

65. आयुर्मर्माणि रक्षति ॥
ఆయుర్మర్మాణి రక్షతి॥
Duration of life preserves the vital parts.

निमग्नस्य पयोराशौ पर्वतात्पतितस्य च ।
तक्षकेणापि दष्टस्य आयुर्मर्माणि रक्षति ॥
నిమగ్నస్య పయోరాశౌ పర్వతాత్పతితస్య చ।
తక్షకేణాపి దష్టస్య ఆయుర్మర్మాణి రక్షతి॥

Life preserves the vital parts of one sunk in the water, of one fallen from a mountain, even of one bitten by [the serpent] Takshaka. (Hitopadeśa, Book 2.)

66. आयुर्याति दिनेदिने ॥
ఆయుర్యాతి దినేదినే॥
Life goes day by day.

लोकः पृच्छति सद्वार्तां शरीरे कुशलं तव ।
कुतः कुशलमस्माकमायुर्याति दिनेदिने ॥
లోకః పృచ్ఛతి సద్వార్తాం శరీరే కుశలం తవ।
కుతః కుశలమస్మాకమాయుర్యాతి దినేదినే॥

People ask by way of compliment 'Are you in good health ?' How can we be well when our life is waning day by day ? (Kavitâratnâkara 152.)

67. आलस्यादमृतं विषं ॥
ఆలస్యాదమృతం విషం॥

By delay [in using it] nectar [becomes] poison.

68. आशया बध्यते लोकः कर्मणा बहुचिंतया ॥
ఆశయా బధ్యతే లోకః కర్మణా బహుచింతయా॥

The world is bound by desire, fate, and much thinking.

69. आशावधिं को गतः ॥
ఆశావధిం కో గతః॥

Who has reached the limit of his desire ?

70. आशाशा परमं दुःखं निराशा परमं सुखं ॥
ఆశాశా పరమం దుఃఖం నిరాశా పరమం సుఖం॥

Desire upon desire [causes] the greatest sorrow ; contentment, the greatest happiness.

71. आहारे व्यवहारेच त्यक्तलज्जस्सुखी भवेत् ॥
ఆహారే వ్యవహారేచ త్యక్తలజ్జస్సుఖీ భవేత్॥

In eating and in business he who discards modesty will be best off.

(cf. Morton's *Bengali and Sanscrit Proverbs* 805.)

72. आहारोपि मनुष्याणां जन्मना सह जायते ॥
ఆహారోపి మనుష్యాణాం జన్మనా సహ జాయతే॥

Food is provided with the birth of men.

धर्मंच चिंतयेत्प्राज्ञः स्वाहारं नैव चिंतयेत् ।
आहारोपि मनुष्याणां जन्मना सह जायते ॥
ధర్మంచ చింతయేత్ప్రాజ్ఞః స్వాహారం నైవ చింతయేత్।
ఆహారోపి మనుష్యాణాం జన్మనా సహ జాయతే॥

The wise should think of virtue and not of food: food also is created with the birth of men. (Kavitâratnâkara 101.)

इ.

73. इच्छामात्रा प्रभोस्सृष्टिः ॥

ఇచ్ఛామాత్రా ప్రభోస్సృష్టిః॥

The Lord's creation is His mere will.

"He commanded, and they were created." **Psalm cxlviii. 5.**

उ.

74. उत्तमं स्वार्जितं वित्तं मध्यमं पितुरार्जितं ।
अधमं भ्रातृवित्तंच स्त्रीवित्तमधमाधमं ॥

ఉత్తమం స్వార్జితం విత్తం మధ్యమం పితురార్జితం।
అధమం భ్రాతృవిత్తంచ స్త్రీవిత్తమధమాధమం॥

[To live upon] self-acquired property is good, [to live upon] that acquired by a father is middling, [to live upon] a brother's property is low, [to live upon] a woman's property is the lowest of the low.

75. उत्तमा कुलविद्या स्यात् ॥

ఉత్తమా కులవిద్యా స్యాత్॥

The caste-craft is the best.

Every man to his trade.

76. उत्तमा मानमिच्छंति धनमानौहि मध्यमाः ।
अधमा धनमिच्छंति मानोहि महतां धनं ॥

ఉత్తమా మానమిచ్ఛంతి ధనమానౌహి మధ్యమాః।
అధమా ధనమిచ్ఛంతి మానోహి మహతాం ధనం॥

Good men seek honor; middling men seek wealth and honor; base men seek wealth: honor itself is wealth to great men.

77. उत्तमेच क्षणं कोपो मध्यमे घटिकाद्वयं ।
अधमे स्यादहोरात्रं पापिष्ठे मरणांततः ॥
ఉత్తమేచ క్షణం కోపో మధ్యమే ఘటికాద్వయం।
అధమే స్యాదహోరాత్రం పాపిష్ఠే మరణాంతతః॥

In a good man, wrath [lasts] for a moment ; in a middling man, for two hours ; in a base man, for a day and night ; in a great sinner, until death.

78. उत्तीर्णेच जलेपारे नौकया किं प्रयोजनं ॥
ఉత్తీర్ణేచ జలేపారే నౌకయా కిం ప్రయోజనం॥

After the stream has been crossed what is the use of the boat on the other side ?

79. उत्पथं प्रतिपन्नस्य परित्यागो विधीयते ॥
ఉత్పథం ప్రతిపన్నస్య పరిత్యాగో విధీయతే॥

The forsaking of one who has gone out of the right way is enjoined.

80. उत्पद्यंते प्रलीयंते दरिद्राणां मनोरथाः ॥
ఉత్పద్యంతే ప్రలీయంతే దరిద్రాణాం మనోరథాః॥

The desires of the poor spring up and perish.

81. उत्साहस्साहसं धैर्यं बुद्धिश्शक्तिः पराक्रमः ।
षडेते यत्र तिष्ठंति तत्र देवोपि तिष्ठति ॥
ఉత్సాహస్సాహసం ధైర్యం బుద్ధిశ్శక్తిః పరాక్రమః।
షడేతే యత్ర తిష్ఠంతి తత్ర దేవోపి తిష్ఠతి॥

Perseverance, daring, courage, wisdom, strength and valour—where these six are, there is God.

82. उदरनिमित्तो बहुकृतवेषः ॥
ఉదరనిమిత్తో బహుకృతవేషః॥

For the belly's sake many disguises are assumed.

जटिलो मुंडी लुंचितकेशः काषायांबर बहुकृतवेषः ।
पश्यन्नपिच न पश्यति मूढोह्युदरनिमित्तो बहुकृतवेषः ॥
జటిలో ముండీ లుంచితకేశః కాషాయాంబర బహుకృతవేషః।
పశ్యన్నపిచ న పశ్యతి మూఢోహ్యుదరనిమిత్తో బహుకృతవేషః॥

With matted hair, with shaven head, with cropped hair, or in the honored garb of red-dyed clothes, the fool, [though apparently] seeing, sees not [Brahma] :— for the belly's sake many disguises are assumed. (Châturdaśamanjarikâstotra.)

83. उद्योगः पुरुषलक्षणं ॥
ఉద్యోగః పురుషలక్షణం॥

Endeavour makes the man.

84. उद्योगिनं पुरुषसिंहमुपैति लक्ष्मीः ॥
ఉద్యోగినం పురుషసింహముపైతి లక్ష్మీః॥

Fortune favors the persevering and stout-hearted.

उद्योगिनं पुरुषसिंहमुपैति लक्ष्मीः
दैवेन देयमिति कापुरुषा वदंति ।
दैवं निहत्य कुरु पौरुष मात्मशक्त्या
यत्नेकृते यदि न सिध्यति कोत्र दोषः ॥
ఉద్యోగినం పురుషసింహముపైతి లక్ష్మీః
దైవేన దేయమితి కాపురుషా వదంతి।
దైవం నిహత్య కురు పౌరుష మాత్మశక్త్యా
యత్నేకృతే యది న సిధ్యతి కోత్ర దోషః॥

Fortune favors the persevering and stout-hearted man. Wretched creatures say "Destiny must give us." Regard not destiny but exercise all your powers ; if your endeavours fail, what fault will there be ?

85. उपकारेण नीचानामपकारोहि जायते ।
पयः पानं भुजंगानां केवलं विषवर्धनं ॥
ఉపకారేణ నీచానామపకారోహి జాయతే।
పయః పానం భుజంగానాం కేవలం విషవర్ధనం॥

By doing good to base men, evil results; the drinking of milk is to snakes only an increasing of poison.

86. उपायेनहि यच्छक्यं नतच्छक्यं पराक्रमैः ॥
ఉపాయేనహి యచ్ఛక్యం నతచ్ఛక్యం పరాక్రమైః॥

That which is possible by stratagem is not possible by valour.

(See Hitopadeśa Book II and Böhtlingk's *Indische Sprüche* 1. 498).

87. उपोदकी समायाति तिंत्रिणीमंत्रिणा सह ।
पलायध्वं पलायध्वं रेरे शाकविडंबकाः ॥
ఉపోదకీ సమాయాతి తింత్రిణీమంత్రిణా సహ।
పలాయధ్వం పలాయధ్వం రేరే శాకవిడంబకాః॥

Upodakî comes with his minister Tintriṇî—flee, flee, ye pretended vegetables.

Said of the excellence of the *Upodakî* (Basella Cordifolia) when accompanied by *Tintriṇî* (Tamarindus Indica).

88. उपोषितस्य व्याघ्रस्य पारणा पशुमारणं ॥
ఉపోషితస్య వ్యాఘ్రస్య పారణా పశుమారణం॥

The breaking fast of the fasting tiger is the killing of a cow.

89. उषः प्रशस्यते गार्ग्यश्शकुनंतु बृहस्पतिः ।
मनोजयंतु मांडव्यो विप्रवाक्यं जनार्दनः ॥
ఉషః ప్రశస్యతే గార్గ్యశ్శకునంతు బృహస్పతిః।
మనోజయంతు మాండవ్యో విప్రవాక్యం జనార్దనః॥

Gârgya [says] the dawn is best; Bṛihaspati, the omen; Mâṇḍavya, the victory of the mind; Janârdana, the voice of the Brahman.

Said with reference to fixing a time for setting out on a journey.

90. **उष्णकाले भवेच्छीतं शीतकाले बहूष्णता ॥**

ఉష్ణకాలే భవేచ్ఛీతం శీతకాలే బహూష్ణతా॥

In hot weather, [people say] 'Let there be cold'; in cold weather, 'Let there be great heat.'

91. **उष्णमुष्णेन शीतलं ॥**

ఉష్ణముష్ణేన శీతలం॥

Heat with heat [produces] cold.

Like cures like. (Latin.)*

ऋ.

92. **ऋणं कृत्वा घृतं पिबेत् ॥**

ఋణం కృత్వా ఘృతం పిబేత్॥

Having incurred debt you should eat ghî.

93. **ऋणव्रणकलंकानां काले लोपो भविष्यति ॥**

ఋణవ్రణకలంకానాం కాలే లోపో భవిష్యతి॥

Debt, a sore, and a stain will be effaced in time.

94. **ऋणानुबंधरूपेण पशुपत्नी सुतालयाः ।**
ऋणक्षये क्षयं यांति का तत्र परिवेदना ॥

ఋణానుబంధరూపేణ పశుపత్నీ సుతాలయాః।
ఋణక్షయే క్షయం యాంతి కా తత్ర పరివేదనా॥

Cattle, a wife, children, and a house are the cause of debt; if the debt is cleared, they go to ruin—what sorrow is there in that?

---

* Similia similibus curantur.

ए.

95. एकः पापानि कुरुते फलं भुंक्ते महाजनः ॥

ఏకః పాపాని కురుతే ఫలం భుంక్తే మహాజనః॥

One commits sin, many persons suffer the consequences.

96. एका भार्या सुंदरीवा दरीवा ॥

ఏకా భార్యా సుందరీవా దరీవా॥

One wife; a beautiful woman or a cave.

एको देवः केशवोवा शिवोवा एको वासः पत्तनेवा वनेवा ।
एकं मित्रं भूपतिर्वा यतिर्वा एकाभार्या सुंदरीवा दरीवा ॥

ఏకో దేవః కేశవోవా శివోవా ఏకో వాసః పత్తనేవా వనేవా।
ఏకం మిత్రం భూపతిర్వా యతిర్వా ఏకాభార్యా సుందరీవా దరీవా॥

One god, either Kêśava or Śiva; one place of abode, either in a town or a forest; one friend, either a king or a hermit; one wife, either a beautiful woman or a cave.

(cf. Böhtlingk's *Indische Sprüche* 1. 557.)

97. एकेनैवतु चक्रेण न रथस्य गतिर्भवेत् ॥

ఏకేనైవతు చక్రేణ న రథస్య గతిర్భవేత్॥

A chariot will not go on one wheel.

98. एति जीवंतमानंदो नरं वर्षशतादपि ॥

ఏతి జీవంతమానందో నరం వర్షశతాదపి॥

Happiness attends a living man even after a hundred years.

99. एष्टव्या बहवः पुत्राः ॥
ఏష్టవ్యా బహవః పుత్రాః॥

Many sons are to be desired.

एष्टव्या बहवः पुत्राः यद्येकोपि गयां व्रजेत् ।
गौरींवा वरयेत्कन्यां नीलंवा वृषमुत्सृजेत् ॥
ఏష్టవ్యా బహవః పుత్రాః యద్యేకోపి గయాం వ్రజేత్।
గౌరీంవా వరయేత్కన్యాం నీలంవా వృషముత్సృజేత్॥

Many sons are to be desired; for one at last may go to Gayâ, or may give away a pure virgin, or free a black bull.

औ.

100. औदुंबराणि पुष्पाणि श्वेतवर्णंच वायसं ।
मत्स्यपादं जले पश्येन्ननारीहृदयस्थितं ॥
ఔదుంబరాణి పుష్పాణి శ్వేతవర్ణంచ వాయసం।
మత్స్యపాదం జలే పశ్యేన్ననారీహృదయస్థితం॥

The flowers of the fig tree, a white-coloured crow, a fish's foot in the water, one may see—but not what is in a woman's mind.

Udumbara is the Ficus Glomerata—(See Telugu No. 59.)

क.

101. कं न वशीकुरुते भुवि रामा ॥
కం న వశీకురుతే భువి రామా॥

Whom on earth will a handsome woman not subdue ?

कुंकुमपंककलंकितदेहा गौरपयोधरकंपितहारा ।
नूपुरहंसरणत्पदपद्मा कन्न वशीकुरुते भुवि रामा ॥
కుంకుమపంకకలంకితదేహా గౌరపయోధరకంపితహారా।
నూపురహంసరణత్పదపద్మా కన్న వశీకురుతే భువి రామా॥

Whom on earth will a handsome woman—her body besmeared with saffron paste, a necklace dangling on her fair bosom, bells tinkling on her ankles—not subdue ? (Bhartṛihari.)

102. कः पापिष्ठो ममाधिकः ॥

కః పాపిష్ఠో మమాధికః॥

What great sinner is greater than I ?

103. कथयति संवृतिरेव कामितानि ॥

కథయతి సంవృతిరేవ కామితాని॥

Concealment itself reveals the wishes.

104. कदलीवंध्या काकीवंध्या ॥

కదలీవంధ్యా, కాకీవంధ్యా॥

Barren as a plantain, barren as a crow.

A woman who has one child and then dies is like the plantain which produces one bunch and then perishes ; a woman who brings forth once and is afterwards barren is like the crow which lays eggs but once.

105. करतलामलकं ॥

కరతలామలకం॥

Emblic Myrobalan in the palm of the hand.

To have a thing at one's fingers' ends.

106. कर्तव्यो नातिसंचयः ॥

కర్తవ్యో నాతిసంచయః॥

Great accumulations should not be made.

कर्तव्यस्संचयो नित्यं कर्तव्यो नातिसंचयः ।
अतिसंचयदोषेण धनुषा जंबुको हतः ॥

కర్తవ్యస్సంచయో నిత్యం కర్తవ్యో నాతిసంచయః।
అతిసంచయదోషేణ ధనుషా జంబుకో హతః॥

We should always lay up [for the future], but great accumulations should not be made ; by the folly of excessive hoarding the fox was killed by the bow. (See Hitopadeśa Book I.)

107. कर्ता भोक्ता जनार्दनः ॥

కర్తా భోక్తా జనార్దనః॥

Janârdana is the doer and the enjoyer ?

The merit of offering a sacrifice, as well as the favor of receiving it, is to be ascribed to Janârdana (Vishṇu.)

సంస్కృతలోకోక్తులు.

108. कर्मणा बाध्यते बुद्धिर्नबुद्ध्या कर्म बाध्यते ॥
కర్మణా బాధ్యతే బుద్ధిర్నబుధ్యా కర్మ బాధ్యతే॥

The mind is ruled by fate, not fate by the mind.

कर्मणा बाध्यते बुद्धिर्न बुद्ध्या कर्म बाध्यते ।
सुबुद्धिरपि यद्रामो हैमं हरिणमन्वगात् ॥
కర్మణా బాధ్యతే బుద్ధిర్న బుద్ధ్యా కర్మ బాధ్యతే।
సుబుద్ధిరపి యద్రామో హైమం హరిణమన్వగాత్॥

Fate rules the mind; not mind the fate;—with all his wisdom, Râma pursued the golden deer!

109. कष्टे फले ॥
కష్టే ఫలే॥

From labour, fruit.

The gods sell us everything for our labours. (Latin.)*

110. कांचनात्कर्ममोचनं ॥
కాంచనాత్కర్మమోచనం॥

By gold is [obtained] freedom from [the consequences of evil] deeds.

Through the priests.

111. काकः काकः पिकः पिकः ॥
కాకః కాకః పికః పికః॥

The crow is a crow; the cuckoo is a cuckoo.

काकः कृष्णः पिकः कृष्णस्त्वभेदः पिककाकयोः ।
आयाता मधुयामिन्यः काकः काकः पिकः पिकः ॥
కాకః కృష్ణః పికః కృష్ణస్త్వభేదః పికకాకయోః।
ఆయాతా మధుయామిన్యః కాకః కాకః పికః పికః॥

The crow is black, the cuckoo is black; there is no difference between the cuckoo and the crow: but as the spring nights appear, the crow is a crow, the cuckoo is a cuckoo. (i. e. the distinction between them becomes clear when the notes of the cuckoo are heard.)

When men are tried, their relative worth is known.

---

* Di nobis laboribus omnia vendunt.

112. काकतालफलन्यायः ॥

కాకతాలఫలన్యాయః॥

The crow and the palm fruit.

As a crow happened to perch on a ripe fruit, it fell.

Said of a coincidence.

113. काकमांसं शुनोच्छिष्टं स्वल्पं तदपि दुर्लभं ॥

కాకమాంసం శునోచ్ఛిష్టం స్వల్పం తదపి దుర్లభం॥

The leavings of crow-flesh by a dog are small; that even is not obtainable.

A churl, when asked to give away a little of his food, first said it was crow-flesh; then, on being pressed, said it was the leavings of a dog; and at last swallowed the whole of it and said he had none left.

114. का कस्य परिवेदना ॥

కా కస్య పరివేదనా॥

Who feels pain?

एकवृक्षसमारूढा नानादेशविहंगमाः ।
प्रभातेतु दिशो यांति का कस्य परिवेदना ॥
ఏకవృక్షసమారూఢా నానాదేశవిహంగమాః।
ప్రభాతేతు దిశో యాంతి కా కస్య పరివేదనా॥

Birds of various countries alight upon one tree; but at the dawn, they each go their way—which of them feels pain?

दुर्दूरांतपथश्रांताश्छायां यांति च शीतलां ।
शीतलाश्च पुनर्यांति का कस्य परिवेदना ॥
దుర్దూరాంతపథశ్రాంతాశ్ఛాయాం యాంతి చ శీతలాం।
శీతలాశ్చ పునర్యాంతి కా కస్య పరివేదనా॥

Wayworn travellers come under the cool shade [of a tree;] but as soon as they are refreshed, they start again—which of them feels pain? Kavitâratnâkara 88.)

115. काचः काचो मणिर्मणिः ॥

కాచః కాచో మణిర్మణిః॥

Glass is glass ; a gem is a gem.

मणिर्लुठति पादेन काचश्शिरसि धार्यते ।
यथैवास्तु तथैवास्तु काचः काचो मणिर्मणिः ॥
మణిర్లుఠతి పాదేన కాచశ్శిరసి ధార్యతే।
యథైవాస్తు తథైవాస్తు కాచః కాచో మణిర్మణిః॥

A diamond is trodden under foot and glass is worn on the head; let them be even in that state, glass is glass and a gem a gem.

116. का चिंता मरणे रणे ॥

కా చింతా మరణే రణే॥

What fear is there in death or the battle-field ?

यदि कृष्ण पदे चिंता भक्तिस्ते पदपंकजे ।
विषमे दुर्गमे वापि का चिंता मरणे रणे ॥
యది కృష్ణ పదే చింతా భక్తిస్తే పదపంకజే।
విషమే దుర్గమే వాపి కా చింతా మరణే రణే॥

If we O Kṛishṇa! contemplate, if we have faith in your lotus-like feet, what fear [need we feel] in trouble or difficulty—in death or the battle field ?

117. कार्येषु दासी करणेषु मंत्री रूपे च रंभा क्षमया धरित्री ।
भोज्येषु माता शयने तु वेश्या षट्कर्मयुक्ता खलु धर्मपत्नी ॥

కార్యేషు దాసీ కరణేషు మంత్రీ రూపే చ రంభా క్షమయా ధరిత్రీ।
భోజ్యేషు మాతా శయనే తు వేశ్యా షట్కర్మయుక్తా ఖలు ధర్మపత్నీ॥

In work, a slave ; in business, a minister ; in form a Rambhâ ; in patience, [like] the earth ; in [providing] food, a mother ; in conjugal enjoyments, a courtesan :— is not she who possesses these six qualities, a dutiful wife ?

118. कालः क्रीडति गच्छत्यायुः ॥

కాలః క్రీడతి గచ్ఛత్యాయుః॥

Time sports; life goes.

दिनमपि रजनी सायं प्रातश्शिशिरवसंतौ पुनरायातः ।
कालः क्रीडति गच्छत्यायुस्तदपि न मुंचत्याशापाशः ॥

దినమపి రజనీ సాయం ప్రాతశ్శిశిరవసంతౌ పునరాయాతః।
కాలః క్రీడతి గచ్ఛత్యాయుస్తదపి న ముంచత్యాశాపాశః॥

Day and night, evening and morning, winter and spring, come again and again; time sports, life goes, but nevertheless the chain of desire loosens not.

(cf. Böhtlingk's *Indische Sprüche* 3. 4181.)

119. कालस्य कुटिला गतिः ॥

కాలస్య కుటిలా గతిః॥

The ways of time are capricious.

अप्सु प्लवंति पाषाणा मानुषा घ्नंति राक्षसान् ।
कपयः कर्म कुर्वंति कालस्य कुटिला गतिः ॥

అప్సు ప్లవంతి పాషాణా మానుషా ఘ్నంతి రాక్షసాన్।
కపయః కర్మ కుర్వంతి కాలస్య కుటిలా గతిః॥

Stones float on water; men kill giants; monkeys perform works; the ways of time are capricious.

120. कालो हि बलवत्तरः ॥

కాలో హి బలవత్తరః॥

Time is stronger [than all things else.]

Death awaits all.

(Morton's *Bengali and Sanscrit Proverbs* 871.)

121. कीर्तिर्यस्य सजीवति ॥
కీర్తిర్యస్య సజీవతి॥

He lives, who has acquired fame.

चलच्चित्तं चलद्वित्तं चलज्जीवन यौवनं ।
चलाचलमिदं सर्वं कीर्तिर्यस्य सजीवति ॥
చలచ్చిత్తం చలద్విత్తం చలజ్జీవన యౌవనం।
చలాచలమిదం సర్వం కీర్తిర్యస్య సజీవతి॥

Mind is transitory; wealth is transitory; life is transitory; youth is transitory; all this is fleeting: he [only] lives who has acquired fame.

122. कुपुत्रेण कुलं यथा ॥
కుపుత్రేణ కులం యథా॥

As a family [is ruined] by a bad son.

एकेनापि कुवृक्षेण कोटरस्थेन वह्निना ।
दह्यते तद्वनं सर्वं कुपुत्रेण कुलं यथा ॥
ఏకేనాపి కువృక్షేణ కోటరస్థేన వహ్నినా।
దహ్యతే తద్వనం సర్వం కుపుత్రేణ కులం యథా॥

By the fire generated in its hollow, a single small tree burns a whole forest, even as a single wicked son brings ruin on his whole family.

123. कुसुमे कुसुमोत्पत्तिश्श्रूयते न च दृश्यते ॥
కుసుమే కుసుమోత్పత్తిశ్శ్రూయతే న చ దృశ్యతే॥

The production of a flower in a flower, has never been heard of, nor seen.

A riddle propounded by King Bhoja, through his mistress, to Kâlidâsa. The poet, addressing her, replied—completing the couplet—

बाले तव मुखांभोजे दृष्टमिंदीवरद्वयं ॥
బాలే తవ ముఖాంభోజే దృష్టమింఁదీవరద్వయం॥

O girl! two blue lotuses (eyes) are seen in the lotus of your face.

124. कृतस्य करणं नास्ति मृतस्य मरणं यथा ।
गतस्य शोचना नास्ति एतद्वेदविदां मतं ॥
కృతస్య కరణం నాస్తి మృతస్య మరణం యథా।
గతస్య శోచనా నాస్తి ఏతద్వేదవిదాం మతం॥

There is no doing of a thing done; there is no death for a dead man; there is no [advantage in] grief for that which is passed—this is the opinion of the learned in the Vedas.

125. कृपणस्य धनं याति वह्नितस्करपार्थिवैः ॥
కృపణస్య ధనం యాతి వహ్నితస్కరపార్థివైః॥

A miser's wealth goes by fire, robbers, and kings.

126. कोकिलानां स्वरो रूपं पातिव्रत्यं तु योषितां ।
विद्या रूपं विरूपाणां क्षमा रूपं तपस्विनां ॥
కోకిలానాం స్వరోరూపం పాతివ్రత్యం తు యోషితాం।
విద్యా రూపం విరూపాణాం క్షమా రూపం తపస్వినాం॥

The voice is the beauty of cuckoos; chastity is the beauty of women; learning is the beauty of the deformed; patience is the beauty of ascetics.

127. कोपः पापस्य कारणं ॥
కోపః పాపస్య కారణం॥

Anger is a cause of sin.

128. कोरुक् हितमितभुक् ॥
కోరుక్ హితమితభుక్॥

Who is without disease? He who eats what agrees with him moderately.

Kâlidâsa's interpretation of a bird's cry "*koruk, koruk.*"

129. कोशवान् पंडितः खलु ॥
కోశవాన్ పండితః ఖలు॥

Is not the man possessed of books a Pandit?

130. कौपीनवंतः खलु भाग्यवंतः ॥
కౌపీనవంతః ఖలు భాగ్యవంతః॥

Are not those who have a clout the fortunate?

i. e. Anchorites.

Said jokingly of a stingy fellow.

131. क्रियासिद्धिस्सत्वे भवति महतां नोपकरणे: ॥
క్రియాసిద్ధిస్సత్వే భవతి మహతాం నోపకరణైః॥

Success in an undertaking rests in the strength of great men, not in the means.

132. क्रोडेमनोधावति ॥
క్రోడేమనోధావతి॥

The mind runs to the [mother's] breast.

"The love of native country prevails in all." (Morton).

वासः कांचनपंजरे नृपकरांभोजे स्तनूमार्जनं ।
भक्ष्यं स्वादुरसालदाडिमफलं पेयं सुधाभं पयः ॥
पाटस्संसदि रामनाम सततं धीरस्य कीरस्य मे ।
हाहा हंत तथापि जन्मविटपिक्रोडे मनो धावति ॥
వాసః కాంచనపంజరే నృపకరాంభోజై స్తనూమార్జనం।
భక్ష్యం స్వాదురసాలదాడిమఫలం పేయం సుధాభం పయః॥
పాఠస్సంసది రామనామ సతతం ధీరస్య కీరస్య మే।
హాహా హంత తథాపి జన్మవిటపిక్రోడే మనో ధావతి॥

My residence is a golden cage; my body is stroked by the lotus-like hands of kings; I am fed with the delicious mango and pomegranite; milk, equal to nectar, forms my drink; the repetition of the name of Râma is my constant task in the assembly; I am a clever parrot; yet still, alas! my heart yearns for the hollow of my native tree.

ख.

133. खलः केन निवार्यते ॥
ఖలః కేన నివార్యతే॥

By what can a wicked man be checked?

सर्पः क्रूरः खलः क्रूरः सर्पात्क्रूरतरः खलः ।
मंत्रौषधवशस्सर्पः खलः केन निवार्यते ॥
సర్పః క్రూరః ఖలః క్రూరః సర్పాత్ క్రూరతరః ఖలః।
మంత్రౌషధవశస్సర్పః ఖలః కేన నివార్యతే॥

The serpent is cruel; a wicked man is cruel; a wicked man is more cruel:—a serpent yields to spells and medicines, but by what can a wicked man be checked?

134. खलानां दुर्जनानां च द्विविधैव प्रतिक्रिया ।
उपायान्मुखभंगो वा दूरतो वा विसर्जनं ॥
ఖలానాం దుర్జనానాం చ ద్వివిధైవ ప్రతిక్రియా।
ఉపాయాన్ముఖభంగో వా దూరతో వా విసర్జనం॥

For the wicked and the evil, the remedy is of two kinds;—either to disgrace them by strategy, or to leave them at a distance.

ग.

135. गंडूषजलमात्रेण शफरी फरफरायते ॥
గండూషజలమాత్రేణ శఫరీ ఫరఫరాయతే॥

The Śapharī splashes in even a mouthful of water.

Sapharī is a small fish (Cyprinus Sophore.)—"Said of a low person unduly elated with a small advancement, and so assuming a ridiculous importance," (Morton).

136. गणाद्गृहीता वर्धेत गणस्य तु न किंचन ।
गणप्रदाता हीयेत गणस्य तु न किंचन ॥
గణాద్గృహీతా వర్ధేత గణస్య తు న కించన।
గణప్రదాతా హీయేత గణస్య తు న కించన॥

He who takes from a number will gain—it is nothing to a number; he who gives to a number will lose—it is nothing to a number.

137. गतं न शोचामि कृतं स्मरामि ॥
గతం న శోచామి కృతం స్మరామి॥

I mourn not for the past, I remember [the benefits] done [to me.]

(cf. Morton's Bengali and Sanscrit Proverbs 836.)

Vain repining is unprofitable but gratitude is a duty.

138. गतजलसेतुबंधनं ॥
గతజలసేతుబంధనం॥

Repairing the tank-bund after the water had escaped.

(See ṬELUGU No. 77.)

To cover the well when the child is drowned. (German.)*

139. गतानुगतिको लोको न लोकः पारमार्थिकः ।
सेतौ सैकतलिंगेन नष्टं मे ताम्रभाजनं ॥
గతానుగతికో లోకో న లోకః పారమార్థికః।
సేతౌ సైకతలింగేన నష్టం మే తామ్రభాజనం॥

Following those gone before, people reason not; by making a sand lingam at the bridge, my copper pot is lost.

A man having buried his copper pot to go and bathe at Adam's bridge near Râmeśvaram made a sand *lingam* over it to mark the place; crowds of people following, senselessly did the same, so that it was a hopeless task for the owner to look for his property.

Silly sheep, where one goes, all go. (Spanish.)†

* Den Brunnen decken, so das kind ertrunken ist.
† Ovejas bobas, por do va una, van todas.

140. गता बहुतरा कांते स्वल्पा तिष्ठति शर्वरी ।
इति चित्ते समाधाय कुरुष्व जनरंजनं ॥
గతా బహుతరా కాంతే స్వల్పా తిష్ఠతి శర్వరీ।
ఇతి చిత్తే సమాధాయ కురుష్వ జనరంజనం॥

O beautiful woman! The night has mostly passed, little remains, bear this in mind and please the people.

Said to an actress, who had danced long but received no present.

141. गतो बहुतरः कालस्स्वल्प एवावशिष्यते ॥
గతో బహుతరః కాలస్స్వల్ప ఏవావశిష్యతే॥

Time has mostly gone, little only remains.

Therefore prepare for another world.

142. गुणदोषौ बुधो गृह्णन्निंदुक्ष्वेलाविवेश्वरः ।
शिरसा श्लाघते पूर्वं परं कंठे नियच्छति ॥
గుణదోషౌ బుధో గృహ్ణన్నిందుక్ష్వేలావివేశ్వరః।
శిరసా శ్లాఘతే పూర్వం పరం కంఠే నియచ్ఛతి॥

The wise man deals with virtues and faults as Śiva [dealt with] the moon and the poison; he praises the former with his head and keeps the latter in his throat.

i. e. he does not expose the faults of others, though he praises their good qualities.

Alluding to the 'Churning of the ocean'.

143. गुणिनि गुणज्ञो रमते नागुणशीलस्य परितोषः ।
अलिरेति वनात्कमलं न दर्दुरस्त्वेकवासोपि ॥
గుణిని గుణజ్ఞో రమతే నాగుణశీలస్య పరితోషః।
అలిరేతి వనాత్కమలం న దర్దురస్త్వేకవాసోపి॥

An appreciator of good qualities is pleased with a good man, but no pleasure [is experienced] by the bad man; the bee goes from the forest to the lotus, but not so the frog, though he lives with it.

144. गुणी गुणं वेत्ति न वेत्ति निर्गुण: ॥
గుణీ గుణం వేత్తి న వేత్తి నిర్గుణః॥

A good man appreciates virtue; a bad man appreciates it not.

गुणी गुणं वेत्ति न वेत्ति निर्गुणो बली बलं वेत्ति न वेत्ति निर्बल:।
पिको वसंतस्य गुणं न वायस: करी च सिंहस्य बलं न मूषिक: ॥
గుణీ గుణం వేత్తి న వేత్తి నిర్గుణో బలీ బలం వేత్తి న వేత్తి నిర్బలః।
పికో వసంతస్య గుణం న వాయసః కరీ చ సింహస్య బలం న మూషికః॥

The virtuous man appreciates virtue, the bad man appreciates it not; the stroug man, and not the feeble, understands strength; the cuckoo, and not the crow, feels the influence of the spring; the elephant, and not the mouse, justly values the strength of the lion.

145. गुरुनिंदा अधोगति: ॥
గురునిందా అధోగతిః॥

Reproaching a Guru is the road to perdition.

146. गृहीत इव केशेषु मृत्युना धर्ममाचरेत् ॥
గృహీత ఇవ కేశేషు మృత్యునా ధర్మమాచరేత్॥

You should practise virtue as if death had seized you by the hair.

147. ग्रामैकरात्रं ॥
గ్రామైకరాత్రం॥

One night in a village.

A wandering life.

घ.

148. घृतस्य पात्रमाधारो वा पात्रस्य घृतमाधारो वा ॥
ఘృతస్య పాత్రమాధారో వా పాత్రస్య ఘృతమాధారో వా॥

Does the vessel hold the ghî, or the ghî hold the vessel?

Said by a would-be logician, as he turned the jar upside down, and so lost all the contents.

Applied to foolish argumentation.

च.

149. चंदनं न वने ॥
చందనం న వనే॥

There is no sandal in the forest.

"The sandal tree grows not in every wood—Eminent persons are rarely seen." (Morton.)

150. चटकस्य मांसं भागशतं ॥
చటకస్య మాంసం భాగశతం॥

A hundred shares of a sparrow's flesh.

To make two bites of a cherry.

He'll make nineteen bits of a bilberry.

151. चर्वितचर्वणं ॥
చర్వితచర్వణం॥

Chewing the chewed.

Said of a man repeating a foolish speech.

He harps ay on ae string.

152. चिंता ज्वरो मनुष्याणा ॥
చింతా జ్వరో మనుష్యాణాం॥

Sorrow is the fever of men.

(See Böhtlingk's *Indische Sprüche* 1. 913.)

छ.

153. छिन्ने कर्णे लूने पुच्छे श्वाश्वेव नाश्वो न गर्दभः ॥
ఛిన్నే కర్ణే లూనే పుచ్ఛే శ్వాశ్వైవ నాశ్వో న గర్దభః॥

By slitting the ears and cutting the tail, a dog is but a dog—not a horse, not an ass.

(See TELUGU No. 571, &c.)

సంస్కృతలోకోక్తులు.

ज.

154. जनवाक्यंतु कर्तव्यं ॥

జనవాక్యంతు కర్తవ్యం॥

One should act according to the people's voice.

The voice of the people, the voice of God. (Latin.)*

155. जनिताचोपनेता च येन विद्योपदिश्यते।
अन्नदाता भयत्राता पंचैते पितरस्स्मृता: ॥

జనితాచోపనేతా చ యేన విద్యోపదిశ్యతే।
అన్నదాతా భయత్రాతా పంచైతే పితరస్స్మృతాః॥

He who brought you forth; he who invested you with the sacred thread; he from whom you received instruction; the giver of food; he who saved you from danger—these five are to be remembered as fathers.

156. जन्मप्रभृति दारिद्र्यं दशवर्षाणि बंधनं।
समुद्रतीरे मरणं कश्चिद्भोगो भविष्यति ॥

జన్మప్రభృతి దారిద్ర్యం దశవర్షాణి బంధనం।
సముద్రతీరే మరణం కశ్చిద్భోగో భవిష్యతి॥

There will be poverty from birth, ten years' imprisonment, death on the sea shore, and [then] a little enjoyment.

The divine writing on a skull (See TELUGU No. 1344) picked up by Bhoja Râja; the "enjoyment" was interpreted by Kâlidâsa to be a ride in Bhoja Râja's palankin.

157. जातस्य मरणं ध्रुवं ॥

జాతస్య మరణం ధ్రువం॥

To him who is born, death is certain.

158. जामाता दशमो ग्रह: ॥

జామాతా దశమో గ్రహః॥

A son-in-law is the tenth planet.

A troublesome fellow.

---

* Vox populi, vox Dei.

159. जामात्रर्थं अपितस्य सूपस्यातिथिभ्यः ।
प्रथम परिवेषणे न प्राधान्यं हीयते ॥
జామాత్రర్థం శ్రపితస్య సూపస్యాతిథిభ్యః।
ప్రథమ పరివేషణే న ప్రాధాన్యం హీయతే॥

The pre-eminence of the son-in-law is not diminished by first serving the guests with the pulse cooked for him.

160. जिघांसंतं जिघांसीयात् ॥
జిఘాంసంతం జిఘాంసీయాత్॥

You may kill him who wishes to kill you.

आततायिनमायांतमपि वेदांतगं रणे ।
जिघांसंतं जिघांसीयान्नतेन ब्रह्महा भवेत् ॥
ఆతతాయినమాయాంతమపి వేదాంతగం రణే।
జిఘాంసంతం జిఘాంసీయాన్నతేన బ్రహ్మహా భవేత్॥

You may kill a man on the field of battle who attempts to kill you though he be learned in the Vedanta; you will not by that become a Brahman-slayer.

Self-preservation is the first law of nature.

161. जिह्वाग्रे वर्तते लक्ष्मीर्जिह्वाग्रे मित्रबांधवाः ।
जिह्वाग्रे बंधनप्राप्तिर्जिह्वाग्रे मरणं ध्रुवं ॥
జిహ్వాగ్రే వర్తతే లక్ష్మీర్జిహ్వాగ్రే మిత్రబాంధవాః।
జిహ్వాగ్రే బంధనప్రాప్తిర్జిహ్వాగ్రే మరణం ధ్రువం॥

Fortune rests on the tip of the tongue; friends and relatives rest on the tip of the tongue; suffering imprisonment rests on the tip of the tongue; death rests on the tip of the tongue.

162. जीर्णमन्नं प्रशंसीयाद्भार्यां च गतयौवनां ।
रणात्प्रत्यागतं शूरं सस्यं च गृहमागतं ॥
జీర్ణమన్నం ప్రశంసీయాద్భార్యాం చ గతయౌవనాం।
రణాత్ప్రత్యాగతం శూరం సస్యం చ గృహమాగతం॥

You should praise food digested, a wife whose youth has gone, a hero returned from the battle-field, and the grain which has come to the house.

163. ज्येष्ठत्वंतु न हि ज्येष्ठे ज्येष्ठत्वं गुण उच्यते ॥
జేష్ఠత్వంతు న హి జ్యేష్ఠే జేష్ఠత్వం గుణ ఉచ్యతే॥

Superiority is not in seniority; superiority is attributed to virtue.

164. ज्वरांतेतु विरेचनं ॥
జ్వరాంతేతు విరేచనం॥

After a fever, a purge.

ट.

165. टीका टूकामपेचते ॥
టీకా టూకామపేక్షతే॥

The commentary requires a commentary.

Obscurum facere per obscurius.

त.

166. तंतुदेशं न पश्यामि यत्र भ्राता सहोदरः ॥
తంతుదేశం న పశ్యామి యత్ర భ్రాతా సహోదరః॥

I see not the country where a brother is.

देशेदेशे कलत्राणि देशेदेशे च बांधवाः ।
तं तु देशं न पश्यामि यत्र भ्राता सहोदरः ॥
దేశేదేశే కలత్రాణి దేశేదేశే చ బాంధవాః।
తం తు దేశం న పశ్యామి యత్ర భ్రాతా సహోదరః॥

Wives can be procured in all countries, and relatives as well, but I see not a country where there is a brother born of the same womb.

167. तवाप्यर्धं ममाप्यर्धं ॥
తవాప్యర్ధం మమాప్యర్ధం॥

Half yours, half mine.

Said by a Brahman impostor who was caught repeating sham Mantras.

(See TELUGU No. 2261).

168. तस्करस्य वधो दंडो दासीदंडस्तु मुंडनं ।
भार्यादंडः पृथक्शय्या मित्रदंडस्त्वभाषणं ॥
తస్కరస్య వధో దండో దాసీదండస్తు ముండనం।
భార్యాదండః పృథక్శయ్యా మిత్రదండస్త్వభాషణం॥

Death is the punishment of a robber, the punishment of a harlot is shaving the head; separation *a toro* is the punishment of a wife, the punishment of a friend is not speaking to him.

169. तावच्च शोभते मूर्खो यावत्किंचिन्न भाषते ॥
తావచ్చ శోభతే మూర్ఖో యావత్కించిన్న భాషతే॥

A fool shines so long as he says nothing.

दूरतश्शोभते मूर्खो लंबशाटपटावृतः ।
तावच्च शोभते मूर्खो यावत्किंचिन्न भाषते ॥
దూరతశ్శోభతే మూర్ఖో లంబశాటపటావృతః।
తావచ్చ శోభతే మూర్ఖో యావత్కించిన్న భాషతే॥

A fool looks well at a distance with his flowing garments; a fool shines so long as he says nothing.

Every fool is wise when he holds his tongue. (Italian.)*

A fool, if he holds his tongue, passes for wise. (Spanish.)†

170. तिलतंडुलन्यायः ॥
తిలతండులన్యాయః॥

Sesamum seed and rice.

Though mixed, their difference will always be seen.

---

* Ogni pazzo è savio quando tace.
† El bobo, si es callado, por sesudo es reputado.

171. तृणजलूकान्यायः ॥

తృణజలూకాన్యాయః॥

Like the leaping leech.

Which jumps along holding on by its head and tail alternately, not letting go its hold at one end until fixed at the other.

A bird in the hand is worth two in the bush.

172. तृणाल्लघुतरस्तूलस्तूलादपि च याचकः ।
वायुना किं न नीतोसौ मामयं याचयेदिति ॥

తృణాల్లఘుతరస్తూలస్తూలాదపి చ యాచకః।
వాయునా కిం న నీతోసౌ మామయం యాచయేదితి॥

Cotton is lighter than grass and a beggar is lighter (more insignificant) than cotton—why is he not carried away by the wind? "Lest he should beg of me" [fears the wind.]

173. तृष्णावधिं को गतः ॥

తృష్ణావధిం కో గతః॥

Who has reached the limit of desire?

निःस्वो ह्येकशतं शती दशशतं लक्षं सहस्राधिपो
लक्षेशः क्षितिपालतां क्षितिपतिश्चक्रेशवत्संपदं ।
चक्रेशः पुनरिंद्रतां सुरपतिर्ब्रह्मास्पदं वांछति
ब्रह्मा विष्णुपदं हरिर्हरपदं तृष्णावधिं को गतः ॥

నిఃస్వో హ్యేకశతం శతీ దశశతం లక్షం సహస్రాధిపో
లక్షేశః క్షితిపాలతాం క్షితిపతిశ్చక్రేశవత్సంపదం।
చక్రేశః పునరింద్రతాం సురపతిర్బ్రహ్మాస్పదం వాంఛతి
బ్రహ్మా విష్ణుపదం హరిర్హరపదం తృష్ణావధిం కో గతః॥

He who has nothing wishes for a hundred; he who has a hundred wishes for ten hundred; the possessor of a thousand desires a lakh; the owner of a lakh desires a kingdom; the ruler of a kingdom longs for an empire; the emperor again wishes for Indra's possessions; Surapati desires to be in Brahmâ's place; Brahmâ to be in Vishṇu's; Hari covets Hara's dominion —who has reached the limit of desire?

174. त्यजेदेकं कुलस्यार्थे ग्रामस्यार्थे कुलं त्यजेत् ।
ग्रामं जनपदस्यार्थे आत्मार्थे पृथिवीं त्यजेत् ॥
త్యజేదేకం కులస్యార్థే గ్రామస్యార్థే కులం త్యజేత్।
గ్రామం జనపదస్యార్థే ఆత్మార్థే పృథివీం త్యజేత్॥

You should forsake a man for the sake of your family; you should forsake your family for the sake of your village; you should forsake your village for the sake of your country; you should forsake the earth for the sake of yourself.

175. त्रिशंकुस्वर्गारोहणं ॥
త్రిశంకుస్వర్గారోహణం॥

Triśanku's mounting to heaven.

King Triśanku, a descendant of Ikshwâku, having been exalted to heaven by the power of Viśvâmitra was hurled from thence headlong by Indra, and remained ever after, in mid-air, head down and heels upward! (See Muir's *Sanscrit Texts*, Part I, pp. 100-103.)

The result of ambition—Applied also to a matter kept in suspense, neither settled one way nor the other. (cf. Morton's *Bengali and Sanscrit Proverbs* 810.)

द.

176. दंडो दशगुणो भवेत् ॥
దండో దశగుణో భవేత్॥

A stick has ten uses.

177. दर्दुरा यत्र वक्तारस्तत्र मौनं हि शोभनं ॥
దర్దురా యత్ర వక్తారస్తత్ర మౌనం హి శోభనం॥

Where frogs are the croakers, there silence is becoming.

भद्रं कृतं कृतं मौनं कोकिलैर्जलदागमे ।
दर्दुरा यत्र वक्तारस्तत्र मौनं हि शोभनं ॥
భద్రం కృతం కృతం మౌనం కోకిలైర్జలదాగమే।
దర్దురా యత్ర వక్తారస్తత్ర మౌనం హి శోభనం॥

Cuckoos do well to keep silent in the winter; where frogs are the croakers, there silence is becoming.

178. दशमाता हरीतकी ॥
దశమాతా హరీతకీ॥

Harîtakî is [equal to] ten mothers.

Harîtakî is the Terminalia Chebula; "the tender buds of this tree are formed into galls which are much prized as an astringent medicine and also as a mordant in dyeing." (W. Elliot's *Flora Ândhrika.*) The fruit is used as a purgative.

179. दाता दरिद्रः कृपणो धनाढ्यः पापी चिरायुस्सुकृती गतायुः ।
राजाकुलीनस्सुकुलेन सेव्यः कलौ युगे षड्गुणमाश्रयंति ॥
దాతా దరిద్రః కృపణో ధనాఢ్యః పాపీ చిరాయుస్సుకృతీ గతాయుః।
రాజాకులీనస్సుకులేన సేవ్యః కలౌ యుగే షడ్గుణమాశ్రయంతి॥

In the Kali Yuga men will suffer these six changes: the liberal man will be poor; the miser will be rich; the sinner will be longlived; the good man will be short-lived; the king will be of low birth; and he will be served by a man of high birth.

180. दातृत्वं प्रियवक्तृत्वं धीरत्वमुचितज्ञता ।
अभ्यासेन न लभ्यंते चत्वारस्सहजागुणाः ॥
దాతృత్వం ప్రియవక్తృత్వం ధీరత్వముచితజ్ఞతా।
అభ్యాసేన న లభ్యంతే చత్వారస్సహజాగుణాః॥

Liberality, sweetness of speech, courage, judgment: these four natural qualities are not attained by practice.

181. दानं दातृवशं ॥

దానం దాతృవశం॥

Giving is in the power of the giver.

Giving or not giving depends upon the will of him who has the means of giving.

182. दारिद्र्यदोषो गुणराशिनाशकः ॥

దారిద్ర్యదోషో గుణరాశినాశకః॥

The defect of poverty is the destroyer of a host of virtues.

अंकस्य दोषो गुणसन्निपाते निमज्जतींदोरिति यो बभाषे ।
नूनं न दृष्टं कविनापि तेन दारिद्र्यदोषो गुणराशिनाशकः ॥
అంకస్య దోషో గుణసన్నిపాతే నిమజ్జతీందోరితి యో బభాషే।
నూనం న దృష్టం కవినాపి తేన దారిద్ర్యదోషో గుణరాశినాశకః॥

The poet, who has said that the blemish of a dark spot is lost in the many beauties of the moon, surely did not observe that the defect of poverty is the destroyer of a host of virtues.

Poverty is no vice, but it is a sort of leprosy. (French.)*

183. दाक्षिण्याद्धननाशनं ॥

దాక్షిణ్యాద్ధననాశనం॥

Complaisance empties the purse.

184. दिवा काकरुताद्भीता ॥

దివా కాకరుతాద్భీతా॥

In the daytime she was frightened by the cawing of a crow.

The feigned timidity of a loose woman. (See the *Bhojacharitra.*)

---

* Pauvreté n'est pas vice, mais c'est une espèce de laidrerie.

185. दीर्घश्रृंगमनड्वाहं निर्लज्जां विधवां स्त्रियं ।
शूद्रमक्षरसंयुक्तं दूरतः परिवर्जयेत् ॥

దీర్ఘశృంగమనడ్వాహం నిర్లజ్జాం విధవాం స్త్రియం।
శూద్రమక్షరసంయుక్తం దూరతః పరివర్జయేత్॥

Keep clear of a bull with long horns, a widow without shame, and an educated Śûdra.

186. दुर्जनं दूरतस्त्यजेत् ॥

దుర్జనం దూరతస్త్యజేత్॥

Keep clear of a bad man.

Keep yourself from the anger of a great man, from the tumult of a mob, from a man of ill fame, from a widow that has been thrice married, from a wind that comes in at a hole, and from a reconciled enemy.

187. दुर्जनः परिहर्तव्यो विद्ययालंकृतोपि सन् ।
मणिना भूषितस्सर्पः किमसौ न भयंकरः ॥

దుర్జనః పరిహర్తవ్యో విద్యయాలంకృతోపి సన్।
మణినా భూషితస్సర్పః కిమసౌ న భయంకరః॥

Though he be adorned with learning, a bad man is to be shunned; is a snake adorned with a gem not to be feared?

A jewel called *Sarpamaṇi* (snake-stone) is said to be found in the head of a snake.

188. दुर्जनः प्रथमं पूज्यस्सज्जनस्तदनंतरं ।
पदप्रक्षालनं पूर्वं मुखप्रक्षालनं परं ॥

దుర్జనః ప్రథమం పూజ్యస్సజ్జనస్తదనంతరం।
పదప్రక్షాలనం పూర్వం ముఖప్రక్షాలనం పరం॥

The bad man to be honored first and the good man afterwards; the feet to be washed first, and the mouth afterwards.

189. दुर्जनः प्रियवादी च नैतद्विश्वासकारणं ।
मधु तिष्ठति जिह्वाग्रे हृदये तु हलाहलं ॥
దుర్జనః ప్రియవాదీ చ నైతద్విశ్వాసకారణం।
మధు తిష్ఠతి జిహ్వాగ్రే హృదయే తు హాలాహాలం॥

Though a bad man speak soft words, that is no ground for confidence in him; it is honey on the tip of the tongue and poison in the heart.

(See TELUGU, No. 4, &c.)

190. दुर्बलस्य बलं राजा बालानां रोदनं बलं ॥
దుర్బలస్య బలం రాజా బాలానాం రోదనం బలం॥

The king is the strength of the weak, crying is the strength of children.

Because they obtain what they want by it.

191. दुर्भिक्षमल्पं स्मरणं चिराय ॥
దుర్భిక్షమల్పం స్మరణం చిరాయ॥

Famine for a short time, the remembrance of it long.

(See Morton's *Bengali and Sanscrit Proverbs* 830).

192. दुष्टा भार्या शठं मित्रं भृत्योहंकारसंयुतः ।
ससर्पे च गृहे वासो मृत्युरेव न संशयः ॥
దుష్టా భార్యా శఠం మిత్రం భృత్యోహంకారసంయుతః
ససర్పే చ గృహే వాసో మృత్యురేవ న సంశయః॥

A wicked wife, a false friend, a servant with pride, living in a house with a snake are [causes of] death, without doubt.

193. दूरस्थाः पर्वता रम्यास्समीपस्थास्तु बर्बराः ॥
దూరస్థాః పర్వతా రమ్యాస్సమీపస్థాస్తు బర్బరాః॥

Mountains are beautiful at a distance, rugged when near.

(See TELUGU, No. 1181.)

194. दूषकश्च क्रियाशून्यो निकृष्टो दीर्घकोपनः ।
चत्वारः कर्मचंडाला जातिचंडाल उत्तमः ॥
దూషకశ్చ క్రియాశూన్యో నికృష్టో దీర్ఘకోపనః।
చత్వారః కర్మచండాలా జాతిచండాల ఉత్తమః॥

A foul mouthed man, a man without employment, a low fellow, a revengeful man — these four are base from their evil deeds; the base-born are better.

195. दृष्टिपूतं न्यसेत्पादं वस्त्रपूतं जलं पिबेत् ।
सत्यपूतां वदेद्वाचं मनःपूतं समाचरेत् ॥
దృష్టిపూతం న్యసేత్పాదం వస్త్రపూతం జలం పిబేత్।
సత్యపూతాం వదేద్వాచం మనఃపూతం సమాచరేత్॥

The foot should be placed [on a spot] seen to be clean, water should be drunk after having been strained through a cloth; a word should be spoken with truth, [a business] should be done with consideration.

196. दैवं पुरुषरूपेण ॥
దైవం పురుషరూపేణ॥

God in the form of man.

God works through men, as His instruments.

197. दैवस्य चित्रागतिः ॥
దైవస్య చిత్రాగతిః॥

Various are the ways of fortune.

198. दैवाधीनं जगत्सर्वं मंत्राधीनं तु दैवतं ।
तन्मंत्रं ब्राह्मणाधीनं ब्राह्मणो मम देवता ॥
దైవాధీనం జగత్సర్వం మంత్రాధీనం తు దైవతం।
తన్మంత్రం బ్రాహ్మణాధీనం బ్రాహ్మణో మమ దేవతా॥

The whole world is subject to God, God is subject to a Mantra, that Mantra is subject to the Brahman, the Brahman is my god.

199. दैवे बले दुर्बले ॥
దైవే బలే దుర్బలే॥

When fortune fails, [nothing can be done.]

200. दोषा वाच्या गुरोरपि ॥
దోషా వాచ్యా గురోరపి॥

The defects, even of a Guru, should be told.

शत्रोरपि गुणा वाच्या दोषा वाच्या गुरोरपि ।
सर्वदा सर्वयत्नेन पुत्रे शिष्ये हितं वदेत् ॥
శత్రోరపి గుణా వాచ్యా దోషా వాచ్యా గురోరపి।
సర్వదా సర్వయత్నేన పుత్రే శిష్యే హితం వదేత్॥

Virtues, even in an enemy, should be acknowledged ; defects, even in a Guru, ought to be pointed out : always, and with all endeavour, should the son and the scholar be taught wisdom.

201. द्रव्यं मूल्येन शुध्यति ॥
ద్రవ్యం మూల్యేన శుధ్యతి॥

A thing is valued for its price.

फलं तु चालनाच्छुध्येत् गोमयेन गृहं तथा ।
चारयोगेन वस्त्रं च द्रव्यं मूल्येन शुध्यति ॥
ఫలం తు క్షాలనాచ్ఛుధ్యేత్ గోమయేన గృహం తథా।
క్షారయోగేన వస్త్రం చ ద్రవ్యం మూల్యేన శుధ్యతి॥

A fruit becomes purified by washing ; so a house by cow-dung ; and a cloth by the use of fuller's earth ; a thing is valued for its price.

ध.

202. **धनमूलमिदं जगत् ॥**
ధనమూలమిదం జగత్॥

In this world, money is the means.

203. **धर्मं च चिंतयेत्प्राज्ञः ॥**
ధర్మం చ చింతయేత్ప్రాజ్ఞః॥

A wise man should think of virtue.

204. **धर्मस्य सूक्ष्मा गतिः ॥**
ధర్మస్య సూక్ష్మా గతిః॥

The way of justice is mysterious.

यातः क्ष्मामखिलां प्रदाय हरये पातालमूलं बलिः ।
सक्तुप्रस्थविसर्जनात्सच मुनिस्स्वर्गं समारोपितः ॥
आबाल्यादसती सती सुरपुरीं कुंती समारोहयत् ।
हा सीता पतिदेवतागमदधो धर्मस्य सूक्ष्मा गतिः ॥
యాతః క్ష్మామఖిలాం ప్రదాయ హరయే పాతాలమూలం బలిః।
సక్తుప్రస్థవిసర్జనాత్సచ మునిస్స్వర్గం సమారోపితః॥
ఆబాల్యాదసతీ సతీ సురపురీం కుంతీ సమారోహయత్।
హా సీతా పతిదేవతాగమదధో ధర్మస్య సూక్ష్మా గతిః॥

Making over all the earth to Hari, Bali went down to the bottom of Pâtâla; with the offering of a measure of flour of fried corn, the celebrated Rishi [Kuchela] procured his elevation to Heaven; in spite of her unchaste character from youth, Kunti rose to the region of angels; while, alas, Sitâ, in spite of her devotion to her husband, went down [into the earth];—the way of justice is mysterious.

205. धर्मो वर्धति वर्धति ॥

ధర్మో వర్ధతి వర్ధతి॥

Virtue increases and increases.

206. धारां तु पश्यति न कश्चन योगसिद्धः ॥

ధారాం తు పశ్యతి న కశ్చన యోగసిద్ధః॥

No gifted Yogi can see the stream.

आनंदतांडवपुरे द्रविडस्य गेहे ।
चित्रं वशिष्ठवनितासममाज्यपात्रम् ॥
हा हंत हंत परिनर्तति तत्र दर्वी ।
धारां तु पश्यति न कश्चन योगसिद्धः ॥

ఆనందతాండవపురే ద్రవిడస్య గేహే।
చిత్రం వశిష్ఠవనితాసమమాజ్యపాత్రం॥
హా హంత హంత పరినర్తతి తత్ర దర్వీ।
ధారాం తు పశ్యతి న కశ్చన యోగసిద్ధః॥

In the city of Anandatâṇḍava, in the house of a Draviḍa, there is a wonder—the ghî pot is like Vaśishṭha's wife, the spoon dances in it; Aha! Aha! no gifted Yogi can see the stream.

(See TELUGU No. 2411.)

Vaśishṭha's wife, Arundhatî, is the personification of one of the Pleiades. The allusion here is to the smallness of the star.

207. धूर्तैर्जगद्वंच्यते ॥

ధూర్తైర్జగద్వంచ్యతే॥

The world is deceived by the wicked.

208. धैर्यं सर्वत्र साधकं ॥

ధైర్యం సర్వత్ర సాధకం॥

Courage is in all things a means [of success.]

न.

209. नंदो राजा भविष्यति ॥

నందో రాజా భవిష్యతి॥

Nanda will become a king.

210. न गृहं गृहमित्याहुर्गृहिणी गृहमुच्यते ॥

న గృహం గృహమిత్యాహుర్గృహిణీ గృహముచ్యతే॥

It is not a house they call the house, but the housewife.

न गृहं गृहमित्याहुर्गृहिणी गृहमुच्यते ।
तया हि सहितस्सर्वान् पुरुषार्थान् समश्नुते ॥

న గృహం గృహమిత్యాహుర్గృహిణీ గృహముచ్యతే।
తయా హి సహితస్సర్వాన్ పురుషార్థాన్ సమశ్నుతే॥

It is not a house they call the house but the housewife; one possessed of her enjoys all the pleasures man is capable of.

211. न च दैवात्परं बलं ॥

న చ దైవాత్పరం బలం॥

There is no power greater than that of fate.

न च विद्यासमो बंधुर्न च व्याधिसमो रिपुः ।
न चापत्यसमः स्नेहो न च दैवात्परं बलं ॥

న చ విద్యాసమో బంధుర్న చ వ్యాధిసమో రిపుః।
న చాపత్యసమః స్నేహో న చ దైవాత్పరం బలం॥

No relative is equal to learning; no enemy is equal to disease; no affection is equal to that for a child; there is no power greater than that of fate.

212. न च धनगर्वितबांधवशरणं ॥
న చ ధనగర్వితబాంధవశరణం॥

Be not dependent on a purse-proud relation.

वरमसिधारा तरुतलवासो वरमिह भिक्षा वरमुपवासः ।
वरमपि घोरे नरके पतनं न च धनगर्वितबांधवशरणं ॥
వరమసిధారా తరుతలవాసో వరమిహ భిక్షా వరముపవాసః।
వరమపి ఘోరే నరకే పతనం న చ ధనగర్వితబాంధవశరణం॥

Better is the edge of a sword, or to live under a tree—better is it to beg, to starve, or even to fall into the dreadful hell, than to depend on a purse-proud relation.

213. न चलति खलु वाक्यं सज्जनानां कदाचित् ॥
న చలతి ఖలు వాక్యం సజ్జనానాం కదాచిత్॥

The words of the good will surely never fail.

उदयति यदि भानुः पश्चिमे दिग्विभागे ।
विकसति यदि पद्मः पर्वतानां शिखाग्रे ॥
प्रचलति यदि मेरुः शीततां याति वह्निः ।
नचलति खलु वाक्यं सज्जनानां कदाचित् ॥
ఉదయతి యది భానుః పశ్చిమే దిగ్విభాగే।
వికసతి యది పద్మః పర్వతానాం శిఖాగ్రే॥
ప్రచలతి యది మేరుః శీతతాం యాతి వహ్నిః।
నచలతి ఖలు వాక్యం సజ్జనానాం కదాచిత్॥

Even if the sun should rise in the west, even if the lotus should bloom on the peaks of the mountains, even if Meru should shake, even if fire should feel cold,—the words of the good will surely never fail.

214. नदीनां सागरो गतिः ॥
నదీనాం సాగరో గతిః॥

The ocean is the course of rivers.

Death is the common lot of all. (Latin.)*

---

* Mors omnibus communis.

215. न दुःखं पंचभिस्सह ॥
న దుఃఖం పంచభిస్సహ॥

With five [others] there is no sorrow.

स्थातव्यं पंचभिःसार्थं गंतव्यं पंचभिस्सह ।
भोक्तव्यं पंचभिस्सार्थं न दुःखं पंचभिस्सह ॥
స్థాతవ్యం పంచభిస్సార్థం గంతవ్యం పంచభిస్సహ।
భోక్తవ్యం పంచభిస్సార్థం న దుఃఖం పంచభిస్సహ॥

You should stop along with five [others]; walk along with five [others]; eat along with five [others]; with five [others] there is no sorrow.

Company in distress makes trouble less. (French.)*

216. न देवस्सृष्टिनाशकः ॥
న దేవస్సృష్టినాశకః॥

God is not the destroyer of his creation.

न माता शपते पुत्रं न दोषं लभते मही ।
न हिंसां कुरुते साधुर्नदेवस्सृष्टिनाशकः ॥
న మాతా శపతే పుత్రం న దోషం లభతే మహీ।
న హింసాం కురుతే సాధుర్నదేవస్సృష్టినాశకః॥

A mother curses not her son; the earth suffers not harm; a good man does no injury; God is not the destroyer of His creation.

217. न दोषं लभते मही ॥
న దోషం లభతే మహీ॥

The Earth does not feel evil.

---

* Qui ne souffre pas seul, ne souffre pas tant.

218. न भूतो न भविष्यति ॥

న భూతో న భవిష్యతి॥

It has not been and it will not be.

अन्नदानात्परं दानं न भूतं न भविष्यति ।
अन्नेन धार्यते सर्वं जगदेतच्चराचरं ॥

అన్నదానాత్పరం దానం న భూతం న భవిష్యతి।
అన్నేన ధార్యతే సర్వం జగదేతచ్చరాచరం॥

A greater gift than that of food, has not been and will not be; by food this whole world, animate and inanimate, is sustained.

219. नमंति फलिनो वृक्षा नमंति गुणिनो जनाः ॥

నమంతి ఫలినో వృక్షా నమంతి గుణినో జనాః॥

Fruitful trees bend down, men of wisdom stoop.

The truly great are humble.

नमंति फलिनो वृक्षा नमंति गुणिनो जनाः ।
शुष्ककाष्ठं च मूर्खश्च भिद्यते न च नम्यते ॥

నమంతి ఫలినో వృక్షా నమంతి గుణినో జనాః।
శుష్కకాష్ఠం చ మూర్ఖశ్చ భిద్యతే న చ నమ్యతే॥

Fruitful trees bend down, men of wisdom stoop;—a dry stick and a fool can be broken but not bent.

220. नमंति संतस्त्रैलोक्यादपि लब्धुं समुन्नतिं ॥

నమంతి సంతస్త్రైలోక్యాదపి లబ్ధుం సమున్నతిం॥

Good men bend to obtain the highest elevation, even above the three worlds.

221. न माता शपते पुत्रं ॥

న మాతా శపతే పుత్రం॥

A mother curses not her son.

(See No. 216.)

222. नराणां नापितो धूर्तः ॥
నరాణాం నాపితో ధూర్తః॥

Among men a barber is the [greatest] knave.

223. नव नव वयं पंच ॥
నవ నవ వయం పంచ॥

Nine, Nine—we [know] five.

When on one occasion, a voice was heard crying "*Nava, Nava,*" Kâlidâsa replied "we [only know] five [grammars].

224. न विद्या कारणं पुंसां भाग्यमेव हि कारणं ।
पाषाणस्य कुतो विद्या देवत्वमुपतिष्ठते ॥
న విద్యా కారణం పుంసాం భాగ్యమేవ హి కారణం।
పాషాణస్య కుతో విద్యా దేవత్వముపతిష్ఠతే॥

The learning of men is not a cause [of greatness]; what learning has a stone? but it obtains divinity.

(See TELUGU No. 2063.)

225. नष्टस्य कान्या गतिः ॥
నష్టస్య కాన్యా గతిః॥

What other resource has a ruined man?

भिक्षो मांसनिषेवणं किमुचितं किं तेन मद्यं विना ।
मद्यं चापि तव प्रियं प्रियमहो वारांगनाभिस्सह ।
वेश्याप्यर्थरुचिः कुतस्तव धनं द्यूतेन चौर्येण वा ।
चौर्यद्यूतपरिश्रमोस्ति भवतो नष्टस्य कान्या गतिः ॥
భిక్షో మాంసనిషేవణం కిముచితం కిం తేన మద్యం వినా।
మద్యం చాపి తవ ప్రియం ప్రియమహో వారాంగనాభిస్సహ।
వేశ్యాప్యర్థరుచిః కుతస్తవ ధనం ద్యూతేన చౌర్యేణ వా।
చౌర్యద్యూతపరిశ్రమోస్తి భవతో నష్టస్య కాన్యా గతిః॥

"Is it right, Hermit, to eat flesh?" "What is the use of it without liquor?" "You like liquor, too?" "Aha! I like it in the company of harlots." "A harlot is fond of money and how can you get it?" "Either by gambling or by theft." "Are you accustomed to gamble and steal?" "What other resource has a ruined man?"

226. न स्त्री स्वातंत्र्यमर्हति ॥
న స్త్రీ స్వాతంత్ర్య మర్హతి॥

A woman is not fit for independence.

227. न हिंसां कुरुते साधुः ॥
న హింసాం కురుతే సాధుః॥

A good man does no injury.

228. न हि प्रमाणं जंतूनामुत्तरक्षणजीवने ॥
న హి ప్రమాణం జంతూనాముత్తరక్షణజీవనే॥

There is no law for living beings of life for the next moment.

(See TELUGU No. 1963.)

229. न हि सर्वस्सर्वं जानाति ॥
న హి సర్వస్సర్వం జానాతి॥

No one knows everything.

230. न हि सर्वे भवादृशाः ॥
న హి సర్వే భవాదృశాః॥

All are not like you.

231. न हि सुखं दुःखैर्विना लभ्यते ॥
న హి సుఖం దుఃఖైర్వినా లభ్యతే॥

No pleasure is obtained without pain.

No rose without a thorn.

232. नानृतं वदेत् ॥
నానృతం వదేత్॥

A lie should not be told.

233. नानृतात्पातकं परं ॥

నానృతాత్పాతకం పరం॥

There is no greater sin than a lie.

234. नारद: कलहप्रिय: ॥

నారదః కలహప్రియః॥

Nârada was a lover of strife.

The Muni Nârada had a knack of sowing discord between others.

235. नारीणां भूषणं पति: ॥

నారీణాం భూషణం పతిః॥

A husband is the ornament of women.

236. नाविष्णु: पृथिवीपति: ॥

నావిష్ణుః పృథివీపతిః॥

There is no king who is not Vishṇu.

i. e. in whom divinity does not dwell.

(See No. 196.)

237. नास्ति ग्राम: कुतस्सीमा ॥

నాస్తి గ్రామః కుతస్సీమా॥

There is no village—how can there be a boundary?

नास्ति ग्राम: कुतस्सीमा नास्ति विद्या कुतो यश: ।
नास्ति ज्ञानं कुतो मुक्तिर्भक्तिर्नास्ति कुतस्तु धी: ॥

నాస్తి గ్రామః కుతస్సీమా నాస్తి విద్యా కుతో యశః।
నాస్తి జ్ఞానం కుతో ముక్తిర్భక్తిర్నాస్తి కుతస్తు ధీః॥

There is no village — how can there be a boundary?
There is no learning — how can there be fame?
There is no wisdom — how can there be salvation?
There is no faith — how can there be understanding?

238. नाहंकारात्परो रिपुः ॥
నాహంకారాత్పరో రిపుః॥

There is no greater enemy than self-conceit.

न चापत्यसमस्स्नेहो न च दैवात्परं बलं ।
न च विद्यासमो बंधुर्नाहंकारात्परो रिपुः ॥
న చాపత్యసమస్స్నేహో న చ దైవాత్పరం బలం।
న చ విద్యాసమో బంధుర్నాహంకారాత్పరో రిపుః॥

No love is equal to that of [a parent for] a child; no power greater than that of fate; no relation is equal to knowledge; no enemy greater than self-conceit.

239. नित्यं सन्निहितो मृत्युः ॥
నిత్యం సన్నిహితో మృత్యుః॥

Death is always present.

Death does not blow a trumpet. (Danish.)*

240. नियतिः केन बाध्यते ॥
నియతిః కేన బాధ్యతే॥

Who can control fate?

मातुलो यस्य गोविंदः पिता यस्य धनंजयः ।
सोभिमन्यूरणे शेते नियतिः केन बाध्यते ॥
మాతులో యస్య గోవిందః పితా యస్య ధనంజయః।
సోభిమన్యూరణే శేతే నియతిః కేన బాధ్యతే॥

On the battle field lies Abhimanyu, whose maternal uncle is Govinda, and whose father is Dhananjaya! — Who can control fate?

241. निर्धनपुरुषः पशुः ॥
నిర్ధనపురుషః పశుః॥

A man without money is a beast.

(See TELUGU Nos. 1876, &c.)

---

* Döden blæser ei Lyd for sig.

242. **निर्धनपुरुषस्तूलसमानः ॥**

నిర్ధనపురుషస్తూలసమానః॥

A man without money is like cotton.

i. e. as insignificant as cotton is light.

(See No. 172—also TELUGU Nos. 1876, 2168, 2169.)

243. **निर्वाणदीपे किमुतैलदानं चोरे गते वा किमु सावधानं ॥**

నిర్వాణదీపే కిముతైలదానం చోరే గతే వా కిము సావధానం॥

What is the use of oil to an extinguished lamp? What is the use of care after the thief has gone?

(See TELUGU No. 77.)

When the head is broken the helmet is put on. (Italian.)*

To stop the hole when the mischief is done. (Spanish.)†

Every ditch is full of after-wit. (Italian.)‡

244. **नीचाः कलहमिच्छंति संधिमिच्छंति साधवः ॥**

నీచాః కలహమిచ్ఛంతి సంధిమిచ్ఛంతి సాధవః॥

Base men love contention, good men love peace.

245. **नीचाश्रयो न कर्तव्यः कर्तव्यो महदाश्रयः ।**
ईशाश्रयो महानागः पप्रच्छ गरुडं सुखं ॥

నీచాశ్రయో న కర్తవ్యః కర్తవ్యో మహదాశ్రయః।
ఈశాశ్రయో మహానాగః పప్రచ్ఛ గరుడం సుఖం॥

The protection of the base should not be sought, the protection of the great should be obtained; the great serpent protected by Îśa (Śiva) enquired after Garuḍa's health.

(See TELUGU No. 751.)

246. **नीचो वदति न कुरुते न वदति कुरुते सज्जनः ॥**

నీచో వదతి న కురుతే న వదతి కురుతే సజ్జనః॥

A mean fellow promises and does not; a good man promises not, but does.

---

* Rotta la testa, se mette la celata.
† Recebido ya el daño, atapar el horado.
‡ Del senno di poi è piena ogni fossa.

247. **नीरुजस्य किमौषधैः ॥**

నీరుజస్య కిమౌషధైః॥

Why medicine for a healthy man?

> **दरिद्रान् भर कौंतेय मा प्रयच्छेश्वरे धनं ।**
> **व्याधितस्यौषधं पथ्यं नीरुजस्य किमौषधैः ॥**
> దరిద్రాన్ భర కౌంతేయ మా ప్రయచ్ఛేశ్వరే ధనం।
> వ్యాధితస్యౌషధం పథ్యం నీరుజస్య కిమౌషధైః॥

Support the needy, O son of Kunti! bestow not your riches on the wealthy. Medicine is proper for a patient; why medicine for a healthy man?

248. **नैषधं विद्वदौषधं ॥**

నైషధం విద్వదౌషధం॥

The Naishadham is medicine for the Doctors.

It tests the powers of the learned.

प.

249. **पंडिता मूर्खजीविनः ॥**

పండితా మూర్ఖజీవినః॥

Pandits live on fools.

250. **पंथा वातेन शुध्यति ॥**

పంథా వాతేన శుధ్యతి॥

The road is cleansed by the wind.

> **रजसा शुध्यते नारी काष्ठं शुध्यति तक्षणात् ।**
> **ताम्रमम्लस्य योगेन पंथा वातेन शुध्यति ॥**
> రజసా శుధ్యతే నారీ కాష్ఠం శుధ్యతి తక్షణాత్।
> తామ్రమమ్లస్య యోగేన పంథా వాతేన శుధ్యతి॥

. . . Wood is beautified by chiselling; copper is polished by tamarind; the road is cleansed by the wind.

251. पक्कानां हि वधे सूत वज्रायंते तृणान्यपि ॥
పక్వానాం హి వధే సూత వజ్రాయంతే తృణాన్యపి॥

O Sûta! in killing those ripe [for death], blades of grass even are equal to Indra's weapon.

252. पटाटोपो भयंकरः ॥
పటాటోపో భయంకరః॥

[His] pomp is dreadful.

253. पत्रं पुष्पं फलं तोयं ॥
పత్రం పుష్పం ఫలం తోయం॥

A leaf, a flower, a fruit, water.

Said apologetically by a poor host to a grand guest.

पत्रं पुष्पं फलं तोयं यो मे भक्त्या प्रयच्छति ।
तदहं भक्त्युपहृतमश्नामि प्रयतात्मनः ॥
పత్రం పుష్పం ఫలం తోయం యో మే భక్త్యా ప్రయచ్ఛతి।
తదహం భక్త్యుపహృతమశ్నామి ప్రయతాత్మనః॥

"I accept and enjoy the holy offerings of the humble soul, who in his worship presenteth leaves and flowers, and fruit and water unto me." (*Bhagavad-gita*, 9. 26. Wilkins' trans.)

254. पतितः पर्वतो लघुः ॥
పతితః పర్వతో లఘుః॥

A fallen mountain is [thought] light [of].

" When a person once prosperous declines in circumstances, he ceases to be respected." (Morton 822.)

255. पयसा सिंचितो नित्यं न निंबो मधुरायते ॥
పయసా సించితో నిత్యం న నింబో మధురాయతే॥

The Margosa tree will not sweeten, though it be constantly watered with milk.

256. परप्रतारणे पांडित्यं ॥
పరప్రతారణే పాండిత్యం ॥

Skill in defrauding others.

257. परान्नं प्राणसंकटं ॥
పరాన్నం ప్రాణసంకటం॥

Another's food is distressing to the life.

Dependence on another for one's livelihood is a miserable state of existence.

(See TELUGU No. 2126)

258. परमे ब्रह्मणि कोपि न सक्तः ॥
పరమే బ్రహ్మణి కోపి న సక్తః॥

No one is devoted to the supreme Brahma.

259. परोपकारः पुण्याय पापाय परपीडनं ॥
పరోపకారః పుణ్యాయ పాపాయ పరపీడనం॥

To do good to others is meritorious, to injure others is sinful.

260. परोपकाराय सतां विभूतयः ॥
పరోపకారాయ సతాం విభూతయః॥

The riches of the good are [employed] for the benefit of others.

पिबंति नद्यस्स्वयमेव नांभः खादंति न स्वादुफलानि वृक्षाः।
पयोधरास्सस्यमदंति नैव परोपकाराय सतां विभूतयः ॥
పిబంతి నద్యస్స్వయమేవ నాంభః ఖాదంతి న స్వాదుఫలాని వృక్షాః।
పయోధరాస్సస్యమదంతి నైవ పరోపకారాయ సతాం విభూతయః॥

The rivers themselves drink not [their] water, nor do the trees eat [their own] sweet fruit ; the clouds eat not the crops—the riches of the good are [employed] for the benefit of others.

261. **परोपकारार्थमिदं शरीरं ॥**
పరోపకారార్థమిదం శరీరం॥

This body is for doing good to others.

Our bodies are given to us as the means whereby we may assist our fellow men.

262. **परोपदेशे पांडित्यं ॥**
పరోపదేశే పాండిత్యం॥

Proficiency in advising others.

**परोपदेशे पांडित्यं सर्वेषां सुकरं नृणां ।
धर्मे स्वीयमनुष्ठानं कस्य चित्तु महात्मनः ॥**
పరోపదేశే పాండిత్యం సర్వేషాం సుకరం నృణాం।
ధర్మే స్వీయమనుష్ఠానం కస్య చిత్తు మహాత్మనః॥

Proficiency in advising others is easy to all men; few are the great men who themselves practise virtue.

Every one thinks himself able to advise another.

Nothing is so freely given as advice. (French.)*

Of judgment every one has a stock for sale. (Italian.)†

263. **परोपि हितवान् बंधुः ॥**
పరోపి హితవాన్ బంధుః॥

Though not of your kin, a friend is your [truest] relation.

(See TELUGU No. 909.)

Many kinsfolk, few friends.

**परोपि हितवान् बंधुर्बंधुरप्यहितः परः ।
अहितो देहजो व्याधिर्हितमारण्यमौषधं ॥**
పరోపి హితవాన్ బంధుర్బంధురప్యహితః పరః।
అహితో దేహజో వ్యాధిర్హితమారణ్యమౌషధం॥

One interested in our welfare is a relative, though a stranger; one injurious is a stranger, though a relative; disease is hurtful, though born in our body; medicine is beneficial, though produced in a forest.

---

* Rien ne se donne aussi libéralement que les conseils.
† Del judizio ognun ne vende.

264. **पक्षिवृक्षन्यायः ॥**

పక్షివృక్షన్యాయః।

Like a bird and a tree.

265. **पापात्मनां पापशतेन किं वा ॥**

పాపాత్మనాం పాపశతేన కిం వా॥

What of a hundred sins to sinners ?

गोमूत्रमात्रेण पयो विनष्टं तक्रस्य गोमूत्रशतेन किं वा ।
अत्यल्पपापैर्विपदश्शुचीनां पापात्मनां पापशतेन किं वा ॥
గోమూత్రమాత్రేణ పయో వినష్టం తక్రస్య గోమూత్రశతేన కిం వా।
అత్యల్పపాపైర్విపదశ్శుచీనాం పాపాత్మనాం పాపశతేన కిం వా॥

Milk is spoiled even by a little of cow's urine, what harm does a quantity of it do to buttermilk ? The pure are involved in trouble by the smallest sins, how will even a hundred sins affect those already sinners ?

(cf. Morton's *Bengali and Sanscrit Proverbs* 811.)

266. **पिता च ऋणवाञ्छत्रुर्माता शत्रुरशीलिनी ।**
भार्या रूपवती शत्रुः पुत्रश्शत्रुरपंडितः ॥
పితా చ ఋణవాఞ్ఛత్రుర్మాతా శత్రురశీలినీ।
భార్యా రూపవతీ శత్రుః పుత్రశ్శత్రురపండితః॥

A father in debt is an enemy [to his son]; a mother of bad conduct is an enemy [to her son]; a beautiful wife is an enemy [to her husband]; an unlearned son is an enemy [to his parents].

267. **पितृदुःखं तु षण्मासं मातृदुःखं तु वत्सरः ।**
भार्यादुःखं पुनर्भार्या पुत्रदुःखं निरंतरं ॥
పితృదుఃఖం తు షణ్మాసం మాతృదుఃఖం తు వత్సరః।
భార్యాదుఃఖం పునర్భార్యా పుత్రదుఃఖం నిరంతరం॥

Sorrow for [the loss of] a father [lasts] six months ; sorrow for a mother, a year ; sorrow for a wife until a second wife [comes]; sorrow for a son, for ever.

268. पिशाचानां पिशाचभाषयैवोत्तरं देयं ॥
పిశాచానాం పిశాచభాషయైవోత్తరం దేయం॥

Devils should be answered in devils' language.

269. पुमान् दुष्कीर्तिसंयुक्तो जीवन्नपि मृतोपमः ॥
పుమాన్ దుష్కీర్తిసంయుక్తో జీవన్నపి మృతోపమః॥

A man of evil repute is, though living, as one dead.

270. पुरुषाणामभावेन सर्वा नार्यः पतिव्रताः ॥
పురుషాణామభావేన సర్వా నార్యః పతివ్రతాః॥

In the absence of men, all women are chaste.

271. पुस्तकं वनिता वित्तं परहस्तगतं गतं ।
अथवा पुनरायाति जीर्णं भ्रष्टा च खंडशः ॥
పుస్తకం వనితా విత్తం పరహస్తగతం గతం।
అథవా పునరాయాతి జీర్ణం భ్రష్టా చ ఖండశః॥

A book, a woman, or money, when gone into the hand of another, is gone [indeed]; or it returns worn out, corrupted, or by bits.

272. पुस्तकेषु च या विद्या परहस्ते च यद्धनं ।
समये तु परिप्राप्ते न सा विद्या न तद्धनं ॥
పుస్తకేషు చ యా విద్యా పరహస్తే చ యద్ధనం।
సమయే తు పరిప్రాప్తే న సా విద్యా న తద్ధనం॥

Learning, in the book, is not learning, and money in the hand of another is not money when the time [of need] arises.

273. पृष्ठताडनाद्दंतभंगः ॥
పృష్ఠతాడనాద్దంతభంగః॥

Falling out of the teeth by a stroke on the back.

(See TELUGU No. 1766.)

Applied to inconclusive reasoning.

274. प्रथमकवले मक्षिकापातः ॥
ప్రథమకబలే మక్షికాపాతః॥

Fall of a fly into the first morsel [of food].

Said of an obstruction at the very commencement of an undertaking.

275. प्रयोजनमनुद्दिश्य न मंदोपि प्रवर्तते ॥
ప్రయోజనమనుద్దిశ్య న మందోపి ప్రవర్తతే॥

Without an object in view, not even a fool undertakes [a business.]

276. प्रवृत्तित्वावच्छिन्नं प्रति कृतिसाध्यताज्ञानं कारणं ॥
ప్రవృత్తిత్వావచ్ఛిన్నం ప్రతి కృతిసాధ్యతాజ్ఞానం కారణం॥

Knowledge of the possibility of the act is an inseparable motive to perseverance.

277. प्रक्षालनाद्धि पंकस्य दूरादस्पर्शनं वरं ॥
ప్రక్షాళనాద్ధి పంకస్య దూరాదస్పర్శనం వరం॥

Keeping away from the mire is better than washing it off

278. प्राणमेव परित्यज्य मानमेवाभिरक्षतु ।
अनित्यो भवति प्राणो मान आचंद्रतारकं ॥
ప్రాణమేవ పరిత్యజ్య మానమేవాభిరక్షతు।
అనిత్యో భవతి ప్రాణో మాన ఆచంద్రతారకం॥

Even at the cost of his life, one should preserve his honor; life is transient, honor is as lasting as the moon and stars.

279. प्राप्तकालो न जीवति ॥

ప్రాప్తకాలో న జీవతి॥

He whose time has come, lives not.

नाकाले म्रियते कश्चिद्विद्धश्शरशतैरपि ।
स्पृष्टः कुशाग्रमात्रेण प्राप्तकालो न जीवति ॥

నాకాలే మ్రియతే కశ్చిద్విద్ధశ్శరశతైరపి।
స్పృష్టః కుశాగ్రమాత్రేణ ప్రాప్తకాలో న జీవతి॥

No one dies before his time even though pierced by hundreds of arrows; touched merely by a blade of grass, he lives not, whose time has come.

280. प्रायो गच्छति यत्र दैवहतकस्तत्रैव यांत्यापदः ॥

ప్రాయో గచ్ఛతి యత్ర దైవహతకస్తత్రైవ యాంత్యాపదః॥

Wherever the fate-stricken goes, there calamities generally go also.

खल्वाटो दिवसेश्वरस्य किरणैस्संतापिते मस्तके ।
गच्छन् देशमनातपं द्रुतगतिस्तालस्य मूलं गतः ॥
तत्राप्येकमहाफलेन पतता भग्नं सशब्दं शिरः ।
प्रायो गच्छति यत्र दैवहतकस्तत्रैव यान्त्यापदः ॥

ఖల్వాటో దివసేశ్వరస్య కిరణైస్సంతాపితే మస్తకే।
గచ్ఛన్ దేశమనాతపం ద్రుతగతిస్తాలస్య మూలం గతః॥
తత్రాప్యేకమహాఫలేన పతతా భగ్నం సశబ్దం శిరః।
ప్రాయో గచ్ఛతి యత్ర దైవహతకస్తత్రైవ యాన్త్యాపదః॥

When a bald headed man having had his head scorched by the rays of the sun, seeking a cool place, went quickly under a palmyra tree, there by the falling of a large fruit his head was broken with a noise! Wherever the fate-stricken goes, there calamities generally go also.

ब.

281. बकः परमधार्मिकः

బకః పరమధార్మికః॥

The crane is very virtuous!

Ironically "applied to one of outward decency and pretence of virtue, but inwardly aiming at injury to others." (Morton, 832.)

शनैः शनैः क्षिपेत्पादौ प्राणिनां वधशंकया ।
पश्य लक्ष्मण पंपायां बकः परमधार्मिकः ॥
శనైః శనైః క్షిపేత్పాదౌ ప్రాణినాం వధశంకయా।
పశ్య లక్ష్మణ పంపాయాం బకః పరమధార్మికః॥

Behold, Lakshmana! for fear of destroying life it places its feet softly in the Pampa lake, the crane is very virtuous!

282. बकध्यानं ॥

బకధ్యానం॥

A crane's meditation.

Cranes appear to be meditating when they are ready to pounce on the fish.

Hypocrisy.

283. बद्धमूलस्य मूलं हि महद्वैरतरो स्त्रियः ॥

బద్ధమూలస్య మూలం హి మహద్వైరతరోః స్త్రియః॥

Women are the great root of the firmly-rooted tree of enmity.

Women and dogs set men together by the ears.

A woman's vengeance knows no bounds. (German.)*

* Weiberrache hat keine Grenzen.

284. **बलवंतं चिकित्सयेत् ॥**

బలవంతం చికిత్సయేత్॥

The strongest should be cured.

उपस्थिते बहुविधे रोगे पित्तादि दोषजे।
हीनाहितकरं त्यक्त्वा बलवंतं चिकित्सयेत् ॥
ఉపస్థితే బహువిధే రోగే పిత్తాది దోషజే।
హీనాహితకరం త్యక్త్వా బలవంతం చికిత్సయేత్॥

When there are divers diseases sprung from bile and the like, the strongest (most dangerous) should be cured, leaving alone those less injurious.

285. **बिंदुस्सिंधुस्सिंधुरप्येकबिंदुः ॥**

బిందుస్సింధుస్సింధురప్యేకబిందుః॥

A drop is as the ocean [to the good]; the ocean is as a single drop [to the base].

Referring to recipients of charity.

286. **बुद्धिर्यस्य बलं तस्य निर्बुद्धेस्तु कुतो बलं ॥**

బుద్ధిర్యస్య బలం తస్య నిర్బుద్ధేస్తు కుతో బలం॥

He who is wise, is strong; the foolish man has no strength.

बुद्धिर्यस्य बलं तस्य निर्बुद्धेस्तु कुतो बलं ॥
पश्य सिंहो मदोन्मत्तश्शशकेन निपातितः ॥
బుద్ధిర్యస్య బలం తస్య నిర్బుద్ధేస్తు కుతో బలం।
పశ్య సింహో మదోన్మత్తశ్శశకేన నిపాతితః॥

He who has wisdom, has strength; how comes strength to him who has no wisdom? Consider how the lion Madonmatta was drowned by the hare.

287. **ब्रह्मज्ञानेन ब्राह्मणः ॥**

బ్రహ్మజ్ఞానేన బ్రాహ్మణః॥

By the knowledge of Brahma, a Brahman.

Spiritual wisdom makes the Brahman.

भ.

288. भवेन्नदीनामुदकं प्रधानं ॥

భవేన్నదీనాముదకం ప్రధానం॥

For rivers, water is the chief thing.

289. भक्षितेपि लशुने न शांतो व्याधिः ॥

భక్షితేపి లశునే న శాంతో వ్యాధిః॥

Though an onion was eaten, the disease was not cured.

To eat onions is forbidden by the Hindu Law.

Said when an object has not been gained even though a considerable sacrifice was made to secure it.

290. भाग्यं फलति सर्वत्र न विद्या न च पौरुषं ॥

భాగ్యం ఫలతి సర్వత్ర న. విద్యా న చ పౌరుషం॥

Fortune is fruitful everywhere, not learning nor human efforts.

समुद्रमंथने लेभे हरिर्लक्ष्मीं हरो विषं ।
भाग्यं फलति सर्वत्र न विद्या न च पौरुषं ॥

సముద్రమంథనే లేభే హరిర్లక్ష్మీం హరో విషం।
భాగ్యం ఫలతి సర్వత్ర న విద్యా న చ పౌరుషం॥

At the churning of the ocean, Hari obtained Lakshmi and Hara, poison; fortune is fruitful everywhere, not learning nor human efforts.

291. भाग्यानि पूर्वतपसा खलु संचितानि ।
काले फलंति पुरुषस्य यथैव वृक्षाः ॥

భాగ్యాని పూర్వతపసా ఖలు సంచితాని।
కాలే ఫలంతి పురుషస్య యథైవ వృక్షాః॥

Fortune, acquired by former penance, brings forth fruit to a man in [due] time, as do the trees.

292. भुक्ता राजवदासीत ॥

భుక్త్వా రాజవదాసీత॥

One should eat and sit like a king.

293. भुक्ता शतपदं गच्छेत् ॥

భుక్త్వా శతపదం గచ్ఛేత్॥

After eating, walk a hundred paces.

After eating, either stand, or walk a mile. (Latin.)*
After dinner sit a while, after supper walk a mile.

294. भुजंग एव जानीते भुजंगचरणं सखे ॥

భుజంగ ఏవ జానీతే భుజంగచరణం సఖే॥

O friend! the serpent only knows the serpent's feet.

(See TELUGU No. 1419.)

295. भूते पश्यंति बर्बराः ॥

భూతే పశ్యంతి బర్బరాః॥

Fools learn by the past.

राजा पश्यति कर्णाभ्यां धिया पश्यंति पंडिताः ।
पशुः पश्यति गंधेन भूते पश्यंति बर्बराः ॥

రాజా పశ్యతి కర్ణాభ్యాం ధియా పశ్యంతి పండితాః।
పశుః పశ్యతి గంధేన భూతే పశ్యంతి బర్బరాః॥

A king perceives by his ears, the learned by their intellect; a beast perceives by scent, and fools by the past.

Experience is the mistress of fools. (Latin.)†
Experience is a dear school, but fools learn in no other.

* Post epulas stabis vel passus mille meabis.
† Experientia stultorum magistra.

296. भृंगकीटन्यायः ॥
భృంగకీటన్యాయః॥

Like the bee and the worm.

The large black bee is said to hum round a worm until it makes it, like itself, a bee.—" The similitude is used to point out the entire change produced in the mind of a pupil." (Brown.)

297. भेकी बकबकायते ॥
భేకో బకబకాయతే॥

A frog croaks.

दिव्यं चूतफलं प्राप्य न गर्वं याति कोकिलः ।
पीत्वा कर्दमपानीयं भेकी बकबकायते ॥
దివ్యం చూతఫలం ప్రాప్య న గర్వం యాతి కోకిలః।
పీత్వా కర్దమపానీయం భేకో బకబకాయతే॥

The cuckoo feels no pride in the possession of a delicious mango; a frog is set a croaking by a gulp of muddy water.

298. भ्रमरकीटन्यायः ॥
భ్రమరకీటన్యాయః॥

Like the bee and the worm.

(See No. 296.)

म.

299. मत्तकुंजरसंघातं भिनत्त्येकोपि केसरी ॥
మత్తకుంజరసంఘాతం భినత్త్యేకోపి కేసరీ॥

Even a single lion tears to pieces a herd of mad elephants.

300. मध्ये तिष्ठति माधवः ॥
మధ్యే తిష్ఠతి మాధవః॥

Mâdhava stands in the middle.

When two persons salute each other, it is as pleasing to Vishṇu as if he were himself worshipped by them both.

301. मन एव मनुष्याणां कारणं बंधमोक्षयोः ॥
మన ఏవ మనుష్యాణాం కారణం బంధమోక్షయోః॥

The mind of men is the cause of bondage and release.

It depends upon man himself to obtain final beatitude and release from mundane existence.

302. मनस्येकं वचस्येकं कर्मण्येकं महात्मनां ।
मनस्यन्यद्वचस्यन्यत्कर्मण्यन्यद्दुरात्मनां ॥
మనస్యేకం వచస్యేకం కర్మణ్యేకం మహాత్మనాం।
మనస్యన్యద్వచస్యన్యత్కర్మణ్యన్యద్దురాత్మనాం॥

At heart, in word, and in deed the good are one; in the wicked, heart differs from word and word from deed.

303. मरणांतानि वैराणि ॥
మరణాంతాని వైరాణి॥

Enmities end with death.

304. मर्कटकिशोरन्यायः ॥
మర్కటకిశోరన్యాయః॥

The monkey and its cub.

As the cub clings to its mother, so man seeks divine aid, and clings to his God.—The doctrine of the *Vadagalais*.

(See No. 313.)

305. मर्दनाद्गुणवर्धनं ॥
మర్దనాద్గుణవర్ధనం॥

Pounding improves the disposition.

दुर्जनं कांचनं भेरीं दुष्टस्त्रीं दुष्टवाहनं ।
इक्षुखंडान् तिलान्छूद्रान् मर्दयेद्गुणवृद्धये ॥
దుర్జనం కాంచనం భేరీం దుష్టస్త్రీం దుష్టవాహనం।
ఇక్షుఖండాన్ తిలాన్ఛూద్రాన్ మర్దయేద్గుణవృద్ధయే॥

A bad man, gold, a drum, a bad woman, a bad horse, stalks of sugar cane, sesamum seed, and Śûdras should be beaten to improve their qualities.

A spaniel, a woman and a walnut tree,
The more they be beaten, the better they be.

306. महागजाः पलायंते मशकानां तु का गतिः ॥

మహాగజాః పలాయంతే మశకానాం తు కా గతిః॥

When huge elephants run away, what hope is there for mosquitos?

307. महाजनो येन गतस्स पंथाः ॥

మహాజనో యేన గతస్స పంథాః॥

That is the road which is trodden by the great.

वेदा विभिन्नाः स्मृतयो विभिन्ना तथा मुनीनां मतयो विभिन्नाः।
धर्मस्य तत्वं निहितं गुहायां महाजनो येन गतस्स पंथाः ॥

వేదా విభిన్నాః స్మృతయో విభిన్నా తథా మునీనాం మతయో విభిన్నాః।
ధర్మస్య తత్వం నిహితం గుహాయాం మహాజనో యేన గతస్స పంథాః॥

The Vedas are divided, the Smṛitis are divided, so are Munis' minds divided; the reality of virtue is placed in a cave—that is the road which is trodden by the great.

308. मक्षिका मारुतो वेश्या याचको मूषकस्तथा।
ग्रामणीर्गणकश्चैव सप्तैते परबाधकाः ॥

మక్షికా మారుతో వేశ్యా యాచకో మూషకస్తథా।
గ్రామణీర్గణకశ్చైవ సప్తైతే పరబాధకాః॥

A fly, the wind, a harlot, a beggar, a rat, the head of the village, and the village accountant—these seven are annoying to others.

309. मांसं मांसेन वर्धते ॥

మాంసం మాంసేన వర్ధతే॥

Flesh is increased by flesh.

i. e. by eating it.

310. मातापुत्रविरोधाय हिरण्याय नमो नमः ॥

మాతాపుత్రవిరోధాయ హిరణ్యాయ నమో నమః॥

Salutation, salutation to the gold [which caused] enmity between the mother and the son.

The story runs as follows: A man found, while ploughing, a pot of money. His mother perceiving this from a distance, determined to kill her son and mixed poison with his food; the son noticing that his mother had seen the treasure and fearing that he would be made to divide it with his brothers, killed her with a blow of the yoke and soon afterwards himself died of the poison. The goddess of money then invited a Brahman, who was in a neighbouring tree, plucking leaves for platters, and had seen all that had happened, to appropriate the treasure, but he declined to have anything to do with it.

311. मातृहीनशिशुजीवनं वृथा कांतहीननवयौवनं तथा ।
शांतिहीनतपसः फलं वृथा तिंत्रिणीरसविहीनभोजनं ॥

మాతృహీనశిశుజీవనం వృథా కాంతహీననవయౌవనం తథా।
శాంతిహీనతపసః ఫలం వృథా తింత్రిణీరసవిహీనభోజనం॥

Vain is the life of a motherless child, so is the prime [of a woman] without a husband; penance without quietism is fruitless, so is food without tamarind juice.

(See No. 87—also TELUGU No. 1028.)

312. मानं धर्मो हतो हरेत् ॥

మానం ధర్మో హతో హరేత్॥

Virtue lost, takes away honor.

313. मार्जालकिशोरन्यायः ॥

మార్జాలకిశోరన్యాయః।

Like the cat and her kitten.

The stronger carrying and protecting the weaker; used to illustrate the free grace of God.—The doctrine of the *Tengalais.*

(See No. 304.)

314. मार्जालाभ्यंजनं ॥

 మార్జాలాభ్యంజనం॥

Anointing a cat.

If oil be put on a cat's head, it is said she will scratch herself to death in a week.

Injuring another by indirect means.

315. मुखं पद्मदलाकारं वचश्चंदनशीतलं ।
हृत्कर्तरीसमं चातिविनयो धूर्तलक्षणं ॥

ముఖం పద్మదలాకారం వచశ్చందనశీతలం।
హృత్కర్తరీసమం చాతివినయో ధూర్తలక్షణం॥

A face shaped like the petals of the lotus, a voice as cool [pleasing] as sandal, a heart like a pair of scissors, and excessive humility—these are the signs of a rogue.

316. मुखे मुखे सरस्वती ॥

ముఖే ముఖే సరస్వతీ॥

Sarasvatî is in every mouth.

i. e. all have the power of speech.

317. मुनीनां च मतिभ्रमः ॥

మునీనాం చ మతిభ్రమః॥

The minds of Munis are [sometimes] confused.

जिह्वा टलति धीरस्य पादस्खलति हस्तिनः ।
भीमस्यापि रणे भंगो मुनीनां च मतिभ्रमः ॥

జిహ్వా టలతి ధీరస్య పాదస్ఖలతి హస్తినః।
భీమస్యాపి రణే భంగో మునీనాం చ మతిభ్రమః॥

The tongue of the brave, [sometimes] falters; the foot of the elepnant shakes; Bhîma even is discomfited; and the minds of Munis are confused.

318. मुरारेस्तृतीयः पंथाः ॥

మురారేస్తృతీయః పంథాః॥

Murâri's is the third way.

The poet Murâri's style differs both from that of Kalidâsa and that of Bhavabhûti.

సంస్కృతలోకోక్తులు.

319. **मुसलः किसलायते ॥**

ముసలః కిసలాయతే॥

The rice pounder sprouts.

(See TELUGU No. 1887.)

320. **मूर्खस्य पुत्रो विधवा च कन्या ॥**

మూర్ఖశ్చ పుత్రో విధవా చ కన్యా॥

A stubborn son, a widowed daughter.

कुग्रामवासः कुजनस्य सेवा कुभोजनं क्रोधमुखी च भार्या ।
मूर्खश्च पुत्रो विधवा च कन्या विनाग्निना संदहते शरीरं ॥

కుగ్రామవాసః కుజనస్య సేవా కుభోజనం క్రోధముఖీ చ భార్యా।
మూర్ఖశ్చ పుత్రో విధవా చ కన్యా వినాగ్నినా సందహతే శరీరం॥

Residence in a hamlet, service under a low fellow, coarse food, an ill-tempered wife, a stubborn son, and a widowed virgin [daughter] burn the body without fire.

321. **मूर्खस्य नास्त्यौषधं ॥**

మూర్ఖస్య నాస్త్యౌషధం॥

There is no cure for the headstrong.

शक्यो वारयितुं जलेन हुतभुक् छत्रेण वर्षातपौ ।
नागेंद्रो निशितांकुशेन समदो दंडेन गोगर्दभौ ॥
व्याधिर्भेषजसंग्रहैश्च विविधैर्मंत्रप्रयोगैर्विषं ।
सर्वस्यौषधमस्ति शास्त्रविहितं मूर्खस्य नास्त्यौषधं ॥

శక్యో వారయితుం జలేన హుతభుక్ ఛత్రేణ వర్షాతపౌ।
నాగేంద్రో నిశితాంకుశేన సమదో దండేన గోగర్దభౌ॥
వ్యాధిర్భేషజసంగ్రహైశ్చ వివిధైర్మంత్రప్రయోగైర్విషం।
సర్వస్యౌషధమస్తి శాస్త్రవిహితం మూర్ఖస్య నాస్త్యౌషధం॥

It is possible to stop fire with water, rain and heat with an umbrella, a *must* elephant with a sharp hook, a bull or ass with a stick, a disease with medicines, and venom by the use of various spells; for every thing there is a remedy provided in the Śâstras—but there is no cure for the headstrong.

322. मूर्खस्य मूर्खो गतिः ॥

మూర్ఖస్య మూర్ఖో గతిః॥

A fool's refuge is a fool.

323. मूर्खेण किं भाषणं ॥

మూర్ఖేణ కిం భాషణం॥

What speech with a fool ?

"Talk not much with a fool, and go not to him who hath no understanding." Ecclesiasticus, xxii. 13.

324. मृत्पिंड एको बहुभांडरूपस्सुवर्णमेकं बहुभूषणात्मा ।
गोक्षीरमेकं बहुधेनुजातमेकः परात्मा बहुदेहवर्ती ॥

మృత్పిండ ఏకో బహుభాండరూపస్సువర్ణమేకం బహుభూషణాత్మా।
గోక్షీరమేకం బహుధేనుజాతమేకః పరాత్మా బహుదేహవర్తీ॥

One lump of clay [is moulded] into vessels of many forms, one gold [is made] into ornaments of many shapes ; [all] cow-milk is one though yielded by many cows ; so the one Supreme soul resides in many bodies.

325. मृत्युर्वै प्राणिनां ध्रुवं ॥

మృత్యుర్వై ప్రాణినాం ధ్రువం॥

Death is certain to all living creatures

(See Nos. 120, 214.)

Man is a bubble. (Greek.)*

326. मौनं सर्वार्थसाधकं ॥

మౌనం సర్వార్థసాధకం॥

Silence gains all objects.

Silence is wisdom, when speaking is folly.

Who speaks, sows ; who keeps silence, reaps. (Italian.)†

---

* Πομφόλυξ ὁ ἄνθρωπος.

† Chi parla semina, chi tace raccoglie.

327. मौनमर्धांगीकारः ॥

మౌనమర్ధాంగీకారః॥

Silence is half consent.

Silence is consent.

Who keeps silence, consents. (Italian.)*

He who says nothing, consents. (French.)†

328. मौनेन कलहो नास्ति नास्ति जागरतो भयं ॥

మౌనేన కలహో నాస్తి నాస్తి జాగరతో భయం॥

By silence there is no quarrel, by vigilance there is no fear.

By silence all occasion of strife is avoided, and by vigilance is removed all cause of sudden fear.

Silence seldom doth harm.
Silence is wisdom, and gets friends.

य.

329. यतो धर्मस्ततो जयः ॥

యతో ధర్మస్తతో జయః॥

Where there is justice, there is victory.

जयोस्तु पांडुपुत्राणां येषां पक्षे जनार्दनः ।
यतः कृष्णस्ततो धर्मो यतो धर्मस्ततो जयः ॥

జయోస్తు పాండుపుత్రాణాం యేషాం పక్షే జనార్దనః।
యతః కృష్ణస్తతో ధర్మో యతో ధర్మస్తతో జయః।

Success be to sons of Pâṇḍu, on whose side is Janârdana ; where Krishna is, there is justice ; where justice is, there is victory.

330. यत्र तिष्ठति धर्मात्मा तत्र देवोपि तिष्ठति ॥

యత్ర తిష్ఠతి ధర్మాత్మా తత్ర దేవోపి తిష్ఠతి॥

Where there is a virtuous man, there also is God.

God helps the good.

---

* Chi tace, acconsente.
† Qui ne dit mot, consent.

331. यत्र धर्मो ह्यधर्मेण सत्यं यत्रानृतेन च ।
हन्यते प्रेक्षमाणास्तु हतास्तत्र सभासदः ॥
యత్ర ధర్మో హ్యధర్మేణ సత్యం యత్రానృతేన చ।
హన్యతే ప్రేక్షమాణాస్తు హతాస్తత్ర సభాసదః॥

Where virtue is destroyed by vice, and truth by falsehood, there the courtiers who witness it become themselves depraved.

332. यत्र धूमस्तत्र वह्निः ॥
యత్ర ధూమస్తత్ర వహ్నిః॥

Where smoke, there fire.

Where there's smoke, there's fire.

No smoke without some fire.

Where there is no fire, no smoke rises. (Portuguese.)*

333. यथा पिता तथा पुत्रः ॥
యథా పితా తథా పుత్రః॥

As the father, so the son.

(See TELUGU No. 176.)

334. यथा बीजं तथांकुरः ॥
యథా బీజం తథాంకురః॥

As the seed, so the sprout.

(See TELUGU No. 1977.)

Bad crow, bad egg. (Greek.)†

335. यथा राजा तथा प्रजाः ॥
యథా రాజా తథా ప్రజాః॥

As the king, so the people.

Like king, like people. (Latin.)‡

---

* Onde fogo naõ ha, fumo naõ se levanta.

† Κακοῦ κόρακος κακὸν ᾠόν.

‡ Qualis rex, talis grex.

336. **यथार्थवादी लोकविरोधी ॥**

యథార్థవాదీ లోకవిరోధీ॥

A speaker of truth is the world's enemy.

(See TELUGU No. 320, &c.)

337. **यथेच्छं विहर वृषभराज ॥**

యథేచ్ఛం విహర వృషభరాజ॥

O king of bulls, roam freely at your will.

(See No. 99.)

A phrase used when liberating a bull in obsequial ceremonies. "The sacrifice of a cow or calf formed part of the ancient Śrâddha. It then became typical, or a bull was turned loose, instead of being slaughtered." (Wilson's note on Vishṇu-purâṇa, Book III, Chap. 15.)

338. **यदि किंचिद्वरे दोषः किं धनेन कुलेन किं ॥**

యది కించిద్వరే దోషః కిం ధనేన కులేన కిం॥

If there be a defect in the son-in-law, what is wealth and what is birth?

आदौ तातो वरं पश्येत् ततो वित्तं ततः कुलं ।
यदि किंचिद्वरे दोषः किं धनेन कुलेन किं ॥
ఆదౌ తాతో వరం పశ్యేత్ తతో విత్తం తతః కులం।
యది కించిద్వరే దోషః కిం ధనేన కులేన కిం॥

A father should first look to [the person of] his son-in-law, then to his wealth and then to his family ; if there be any defect in the son-in-law, what is wealth and what is birth?

339. **यदि हृदयमशुद्धं तस्य सर्वं विरुद्धं ॥**

యది హృదయమశుద్ధం తస్య సర్వం విరుద్ధం॥

If the heart be impure, all [the actions] will be wrong.

This can also be rendered "If a man's heart be impure, all things will appear opposed to him."

340. यद्गतं तद्गतं गतं ॥

యద్గతం తద్గతం గతం॥

What is gone, is gone, gone.

(See TELUGU Nos. 2000, 2162.)

341. यद्दिनं तद्दिनं नास्ति तद्दिनं दुर्दिनं मम ॥

యద్దినం తద్దినం నాస్తి తద్దినం దుర్దినం మమ॥

What day is not a "That-day", that day is a bad day for me.

(For *Taddina* [lit. "that day"] see TELUGU No. 271.)

Said by a poor Brahman who lived by attending obsequial ceremonies (*Śrâddha.*)

342. यद्विधेर्मनसि स्थितं ॥

యద్విధేర్మనసి స్థితం॥

As Fate wills it.

करोतु नाम नीतिज्ञो व्यवसायमितस्ततः ।
फलं पुनस्तदेवास्य यद्विधेर्मनसि स्थितं ॥

కరోతు నామ నీతిజ్ఞో వ్యవసాయమితస్తతః।
ఫలం పునస్తదేవాస్య యద్విధేర్మనసి స్థితం॥

Let a politic man certainly attempt this and that, but the fruit shall be as Fate wills it.

" *There's a divinity that shapes our ends,*
Rough-hew them how we will." Shakespeare.

343. यमस्य करुणा नास्ति तस्माज्जाग्रत जाग्रत ॥

యమస్య కరుణా నాస్తి తస్మాజ్జాగ్రత జాగ్రత॥

Yama has no mercy, be careful therefore, be careful!

Yama is the god of death, " the deity of *Naraka* or hell : he corresponds with the Grecian god Pluto and the judge of hell Minos, and in Hindu mythology is often identified with Death and Time." (Wilson.)

344. यस्य नास्ति स्वयं प्रज्ञा शास्त्रं तस्य करोति किं ॥
యస్య నాస్తి స్వయం ప్రజ్ఞా శాస్త్రం తస్య కరోతి కిం॥

Who has no sense of his own, what will the Sâstra do for him?

यस्य नास्ति स्वयं प्रज्ञा शास्त्रं तस्य करोति किं ।
लोचनाभ्यां विहीनस्य दर्पणः किं करिष्यति ॥
యస్య నాస్తి స్వయం ప్రజ్ఞా శాస్త్రం తస్య కరోతి కిం ।
లోచనాభ్యాం విహీనస్య దర్పణః కిం కరిష్యతి॥

What will the Sâstra do for him who has no sense of his own? what will a mirror do for him who has lost his eyes?

What has a blind man to do with a mirror? (Greek.)*

345. यस्यास्ति वित्तं स नरः कुलीनस्सपंडितस्सश्रुतवान् विधिज्ञः ।
स एव वक्ता स च दर्शनीयः सर्वे गुणाः कांचनमाश्रयंति ॥
యస్యాస్తి విత్తం స నరః కులీనస్సపండితస్సశ్రుతవాన్ విధిజ్ఞః।
స ఏవ వక్తా స చ దర్శనీయః సర్వే గుణాః కాంచనమాశ్రయంతి॥

Who has wealth, that man is of high birth, he is learned, he is a hearer [of the Vedas], he has a knowledge of the precepts, he is eloquent, he is handsome—all qualities follow gold.

Ironical.

Money makes the man.

Money is the god of the world.

All things are obedient to money. (Latin.)†

346. यस्मिन् जीवति जीवंति बहवस्स तु जीवति ॥
యస్మిన్ జీవతి జీవంతి బహవస్స తు జీవతి॥

He [truly] lives by whom many live.

He lives a worthy life who supports many lives besides his own.

---

* Τὶ τυφλῷ καὶ κατόπτρῳ.

† Pecuniae obediunt omnia.

347. यस्मिन् देशे यदाचारः पारंपर्यो विधीयते ॥

యస్మిన్ దేశే యదాచారః పారంపర్యో విధీయతే॥

In every country, that custom prevails which has come down from generation to generation.

न दोषो मगधे मद्ये चान्नयोनौ कलिंगके ।
ओड्रे भ्रातृवधूभोगे गौडे मत्स्यस्य भोजने ॥
दुहितुर्मातुलस्यापि विवाहे द्राविडे तथा ।
यस्मिन् देशे यदाचारः पारंपर्यो विधीयते ॥

న దోషో మగధే మద్యే చాన్నయోనౌ కలింగకే।
ఓడ్రే భ్రాతృవధూభోగే గౌడే మత్స్యస్య భోజనే॥
దుహితుర్మాతులస్యాపి వివాహే ద్రావిడే తథా।
యస్మిన్ దేశే యదాచారః పారంపర్యో విధీయతే॥

In Magadha, there is no crime in [drinking] liquor; in Kalinga, in [drinking] arrack; in Orissa, in co-habitation with a brother's wife; in Gauḍa, in eating fish; in Drâviḍa, in marrying a maternal uncle's daughter:—that custom obtains in every country, which has been handed down from generation to generation.

Every country has its custom. (Spanish.)*

So many countries, so many customs. (French.)†

Every land its own custom, every wheel its own spindle. (Portuguese.)‡

348. यादृशः पुरुषस्यात्मा तादृशं संप्रभाषते ॥

యాదృశః పురుషస్యాత్మా తాదృశం సంప్రభాషతే॥

As a man's heart is, so does he speak.

As the life is, so will be the language. (Greek.)§

---

* En cada tierra su uso.

† Tant de pays, tant de guises.

‡ Cada terra com seu uso, cada roca com seu fuso.

§ Οἷος ὁ βίος, τοῖος ὁ λόγος.

349. **यादृशी भावना यस्य सिद्धिर्भवति तादृशी ॥**

యాదృశీ భావనా యస్య సిద్ధిర్భవతి తాదృశీ॥

As is the perception, so is the fulfilment.

Success depends upon faith.

दैवे तीर्थे द्विजे मंत्रे दैवज्ञे भेषजे गुरौ ।
यादृशी भावना यस्य सिद्धिर्भवति तादृशी ॥

దైవే తీర్థే ద్విజే మంత్రే దైవజ్ఞే భేషజే గురౌ।
యాదృశీ భావనా యస్య సిద్ధిర్భవతి తాదృశీ॥

In God, in pilgrimage, in a Brahman, in medicine and in a Guru, as is the perception, so is the fulfilment.

350. **यादृशी माता तादृशी पुत्री ॥**

యాదృశీ మాతా తాదృశీ పుత్రీ॥

Like mother, like daughter.

(See TELUGU No. 1019.)

351. **यावज्जीवं होष्यामि ॥**

యావజ్జీవం హోష్యామి॥

I shall make offerings all my life.

352. **यावन्मुखगतं पिंडं तावन्मधुरभाषणं ॥**

యావన్ముఖగతం పిండం తావన్మధురభాషణం॥

As long as there is food in the mouth, so long will the words be sweet.

(See TELUGU No. 399.)

353. **युक्तियुक्तं वचो ग्राह्यं बालादपि शुकादपि ॥**

యుక్తియుక్తం వచో గ్రాహ్యం బాలాదపి శుకాదపి॥

A reasonable word should be received even from a child or a parrot.

354. **युष्माकं बदरीमूलमस्माकं बदरीतरुः ।**
बादरायणसंबंधो यूयं यूयं वयं वयं ॥

యుష్మాకం బదరీమూలమస్మాకం బదరీతరుః।
బాదరాయణసంబంధో యూయం యూయం వయం వయం॥

Yours is the jujube root, mine is the jujube tree; ours is a jujube relationship—You are you, I am I.

Said by one who had pretended to be a relation.—*Badari* is the Zizyphus Jujuba.

355. येन केन प्रकारेण प्रसिद्धः पुरुषो भव ॥

యేన కేన ప్రకారేణ ప్రసిద్ధః పురుషో భవ॥

In some way or other, become a famous man.

356. येषामन्या गतिर्नास्ति तेषां वाराणसी गतिः ॥

యేషామన్యా గతిర్నాస్తి తేషాం వారాణసీ గతిః॥

For those who have no other resource, Vârâṇasî (Benares) is a refuge.

(See TELUGU No. 2680.)

मातापितृपरित्यक्ता ये त्यक्ता निजबंधुभिः ।
येषामन्या गतिर्नास्ति तेषां वाराणसी गतिः ॥

మాతాపితృపరిత్యక్తా యే త్యక్తా నిజబంధుభిః।
యేషామన్యా గతిర్నాస్తి తేషాం వారాణసీ గతిః॥

For such as are forsaken by their parents and relatives, and have no other resource, Benares is a refuge.

357. योग्यं योग्येन युज्यते ॥

యోగ్యం యోగ్యేన యుజ్యతే॥

Like joins with like.

(See TELUGU No. 735, &c.)

भार्या मे नर्त्तकी चेयमहं च यवनाधमः ।
जामाता षड्डकश्चैव योग्यं योग्येन युज्यते ॥

భార్యా మే నర్తకీ చేయమహం చ యవనాధమః।
జామాతా షడ్డకశ్చైవ యోగ్యం యోగ్యేన యుజ్యతే॥

This my wife is a dancing girl, and I am the lowest of Yavanas; [so are] my son-in-law and wife's brother-in-law : like joins with like.

Like loves like. (Greek.)*

---

* Ὅμοιον ὁμοίῳ φίλον.

358. **यो यस्य हृद्यो न हि तस्य दूरः ॥**

యో యస్య హృద్యో న హి తస్య దూరః॥

What is dear to one's heart is not far off.

(See TELUGU No. 186.)

गिरौ कलापी गगने पयोदो लक्षांतरेऽर्कश्च जलेषु पद्मं ।

इंदुर्द्विलक्षे कुमुदस्य बंधुर्यो यस्य हृद्यो न हि तस्य दूरः ॥

గిరౌ కలాపీ గగనే పయోదో లక్షాంతరేర్కశ్చ జలేషు పద్మం।

ఇందుర్ద్విలక్షే కుముదస్య బంధుర్యోయస్య హృద్యో న హి తస్య దూరః॥

The peacock is in the mountain and the clouds in the sky; at the distance of a hundred thousand yojanas is the sun, and the lotus is in the water; two hundred thousand yojanas away is the moon from its friend, the lily—what is dear to one's heart is not far off.

Kumuda is the white esculent water lily (Nymphæa esculenta) which expands its petals during the night.

र.

359. **राजवत्पंचवर्षाणि दशवर्षाणि दासवत् ।**

प्राप्ते तु षोडशे वर्षे पुत्रं मित्रवदाचरेत् ॥

రాజవత్పంచవర్షాణి దశవర్షాణి దాసవత్।

ప్రాప్తే తు షోడశే వర్షే పుత్రం మిత్రవదాచరేత్॥

A son should be treated as a prince for five years, as a slave for ten years, and in his sixteenth year, as a friend.

360. **राजा मत्तः शिशुश्चैव प्रमादी धनगर्वितः ।**

अप्राप्यमपि वांछंति किं पुनर्लभ्यतेपि यत् ॥

రాజా మత్తః శిశుశ్చైవ ప్రమాదీ ధనగర్వితః।

అప్రాప్యమపి వాంఛంతి కిం పునర్లభ్యతేపి యత్॥

A king, a drunken man, a child, a madman, a purse proud man desire what is not obtainable—how much more that which can be had?

361. राजा राष्ट्रकृतं पापं राजपापं पुरोहितः ।
भर्ता च स्त्रीकृतं पापं शिष्यपापं गुरुर्व्रजेत् ॥
రాజా రాష్ట్రకృతం పాపం రాజపాపం పురోహితః।
భర్తా చ స్త్రీకృతం పాపం శిష్యపాపం గురుర్వ్రజేత్॥

The king must answer for his country's sin; the priest for the king's sin; the husband for the wife's sin, and the Guru for the disciple's sin.

362. राजन् कनकवर्षाणि त्वयि सर्वत्र वर्षति ।
अभाग्यछत्रसंपन्ने मयि नायांति बिंदवः ॥
రాజన్ కనకవర్షాణి త్వయి సర్వత్ర వర్షతి।
అభాగ్యచ్ఛత్రసంపన్నే మయి నాయాంతి బిందవః॥

O king! a rain of gold falls from thee in all places, but no drops reach me, covered with the umbrella of misfortune.

363. रामरावणयोर्युद्धं रामरावणयोरिव ॥
రామరావణయోర్యుద్ధం రామరావణయోరివ॥

The battle between Râma and Râvana is like that between Râma and Râvaṇa.

i. e., like nothing else—nothing can be compared to it.

गगनं गगनाकारं सागरस्सागरोपमः ।
रामरावणयोर्युद्धं रामरावणयोरिव ॥
గగనం గగనాకారం సాగరస్సాగరోపమః।
రామరావణయోర్యుద్ధం రామరావణయోరివ॥

The sky is like the sky, the ocean is like the ocean; the battle between Râma and Râvaṇa is like that between Râma and Râvaṇa.

సంస్కృతలోకోక్తులు.

364. रामाय स्वस्ति रावणाय स्वस्ति ॥

రామాయ స్వస్తి రావణాయ స్వస్తి॥

Blessings on Râma! Blessings on Râvaṇa!

(See TELUGU No. 1853.)

Applied to keeping on good terms with both parties in a quarrel, and not espousing the cause of either.

365. रूपयौवनसंपन्ना विशुद्धकुलसंभवाः ।
विद्याहीना न शोभंते निर्गंधा इव किंशुकाः ॥

రూపయౌవనసంపన్నా విశుద్ధకులసంభవాః।
విద్యాహీనా న శోభంతే నిర్గంధా ఇవ కింశుకాః॥

Though possessed of beauty and youth and sprung from a pure stock, the unlearned shine not, as the inodorous kiṁśuka flowers [are valueless].

Kiṁśuka is the Butea frondosa.

ल.

366. लंघनं परमौषधं ॥

లంఘనం పరమౌషధం॥

Fasting is the best medicine.

Feed sparingly, and defy the physician.

367. लज्जा स्त्रीभूषणं ॥

లజ్జా స్త్రీభూషణం॥

Modesty is the ornament of women.

*"I will therefore that * * women adorn themselves with shamefacedness."* 1 Timothy, ii. 8, 9.

368. ललाटलिखिता रेखा परिमार्ष्टुं न शक्यते ॥

లలాటలిఖితా రేఖా పరిమార్ష్టుం న శక్యతే॥

The line written on the forehead cannot be effaced.

(See TELUGU Nos. 1344, 1037.)

369. ललाटलेखा न पुनः प्रयाति ॥

లలాటలేఖా న పునః ప్రయాతి॥

The writing on the forehead will never fail.

(See TELUGU Nos. 2431, 2450.)

लब्धव्यमर्थं लभते मनुष्यो देवोपि तं वारयितुं न शक्तः ।
अतो न शोचामि न विस्मयो मे ललाटलेखा न पुनः प्रयाति ॥

లబ్ధవ్యమర్థం లభతే మనుష్యో దేవోపి తం వారయితుం న శక్తః।
అతో న శోచామి న విస్మయో మే లలాటలేఖా న పునః ప్రయాతి॥

Man obtains what wealth he is to obtain, even God is not able to prevent it; hence I neither grieve nor am surprised—the writing on the forehead will never fail.

370. लोको भिन्नरुचिः ॥

లోకో భిన్నరుచిః॥

The world is divided in tastes.

(See TELUGU No. 1616.)

व.

371. वचने को दरिद्रः ॥

వచనే కో దరిద్రః॥

Who is poor in speech?

Good words cost nothing, but are worth much.

372. वसंतयौवना वृक्षाः पुरुषा धनयौवनाः ।
सौभाग्ययौवना नार्यो युवानो बुद्धियौवनाः ॥

వసంతయౌవనా వృక్షాః పురుషా ధనయౌవనాః।
సౌభాగ్యయౌవనా నార్యో యువానో బుద్ధియౌవనాః॥

The spring is the youth of trees, wealth is the youth of men, beauty is the youth of women, intelligence is the youth of the young.

373. **वस्त्रेण वपुषा वाचा ॥**

వస్త్రేణ వపుషా వాచా॥

By dress, by body, and by speech.

374. **वाग्दोषेण हता वयं ॥**

వాగ్దోషేణ హతా వయం॥

We are ruined by foolish speech.

(See TELUGU No. 1347.)

375. **वाणिज्ये वसते लक्ष्मीः ॥**

వాణిజ్యే వసతే లక్ష్మీః॥

Fortune dwells in trade.

वाणिज्ये वसते लक्ष्मीस्तदर्धं कृषिकर्मणि ।
तदर्धं राजसेवायां भिक्षायां नैव नैव च ॥

వాణిజ్యే వసతే లక్ష్మీస్తదర్ధం కృషికర్మణి।
తదర్ధం రాజసేవాయాం భిక్షాయాం నైవ నైవ చ॥

Fortune dwells in trade; she is half in agriculture, half of that in Government service, and not at all in begging.

376. **वादभ्रष्टो वैद्यश्रेष्ठः ॥**

వాదభ్రష్టో వైద్యశ్రేష్ఠః॥

A ruined alchymist [makes] a capital doctor.

377. **विद्यया सह मर्तव्यं न चैनामूषरे वपेत् ॥**

విద్యయా సహ మర్తవ్యం న చైనామూషరే వపేత్॥

One should die with his learning, not sow it in a barren soil.

Better that a man's learning should die with him than that it should be thrown away on the foolish.

378. विद्यानाशाय कल्याणं सर्वनाशाय शोभनं ॥
విద్యానాశాయ కల్యాణం సర్వనాశాయ శోభనం॥

Marriage is ruin to learning, and the consummation of marriage is ruin to everything.

379. विद्यारत्नं महाधनं ॥
విద్యారత్నం మహాధనం॥

The gem of learning is great wealth.

ज्ञातिभिर्वंटनेनैव चौर्येणापि न नीयते ।
दानेनैव क्षयं याति विद्यारत्नं महाधनं ॥
జ్ఞాతిభిర్వంటనేనైవ చౌర్యేణాపి న నీయతే।
దానేనైవ క్షయం యాతి విద్యారత్నం మహాధనం॥

The gem of learning is great wealth; it cannot be shared by cousins, nor lost by robbery, nor exhausted by liberality.

380. विद्यावान् धनवान् भवेत् ॥
విద్యావాన్ ధనవాన్ భవేత్॥

The possessor of learning becomes the possessor of wealth.

"*Get learning with a great sum of money and get much gold by her.*" Ecclesiasticus li. 28.

381. विद्याविहीनः पशुः ॥
విద్యావిహీనః పశుః॥

One void of learning is a beast.

विद्या राजसु पूज्यते न हि धनं विद्याविहीनः पशुः ॥
విద్యా రాజసు పూజ్యతే న హి ధనం విద్యావిహీనః పశుః॥

Learning is honored by kings, not wealth; one void of learning is a beast.

382. विद्वानेव विजानाति विद्वज्जनपरिश्रमं ।
न हि वंध्या विजानाति गुर्वीं प्रसववेदनां ॥
విద్వానేవ విజానాతి విద్వజ్జనపరిశ్రమం।
న హి వంధ్యా విజానాతి గుర్వీం ప్రసవవేదనాం॥

The learned only know the labour of the learned, the barren woman knows not the great pains of childbirth.

(See TELUGU No. 807.)

383. विधिरहो बलवानिति मे मतिः ॥
విధిరహో బలవానితి మే మతిః॥

Lo! Fate is all powerful, that's my mind.

शशिदिवाकरयोर्ग्रहपीडनं गजभुजंगमयोरपि बंधनं ।
मतिमतां च विलोक्य दरिद्रतां विधिरहो बलवानिति मे मतिः॥
శశిదివాకరయోర్గ్రహపీడనం గజభుజంగమయోరపి బంధనం।
మతిమతాం చ విలోక్య దరిద్రతాం విధిరహో బలవానితి మే మతిః॥

Seeing the seizure of the sun and the moon by Graha, the restraint [exercised] over elephants and serpents, and the poverty of the wise, lo! I am of opinion that Fate is all powerful. (Bhartṛihari.)

Graha is a name of Râhu, the personified ascending node.

384. विधिविहितं बुद्धिरनुसरति ॥
విధివిహితం బుద్ధిరనుసరతి॥

Mind follows what Fate has decreed.

385. विनाशकाले विपरीतबुद्धिः ॥
వినాశకాలే విపరీతబుద్ధిః॥

In the time of calamity, the sense is perverted.

386. विपदस्संतु नश्शश्वद्यासु संस्मर्यते हरिः ॥
విపదస్సంతు నశ్శశ్వద్యాసు సంస్మర్యతే హరిః॥

Let misfortunes come upon us often, by which Hari (Vishṇu) is remembered.

387. विपदि धैर्यमथाभ्युदये क्षमा सदसि वाक्पटुता युधि विक्रमः ।
यशसि चाभिरतिर्व्यसनं श्रुतौ प्रकृतिसिद्धमिदं हि महात्मनां ॥

విపది ధైర్యమథాభ్యుదయే క్షమా సదసి వాక్పటుతా యుధి విక్రమః।
యశసి చాభిరతిర్వ్యసనం శ్రుతౌ ప్రకృతిసిద్ధమిదం హి మహాత్మనాం॥

Fortitude in misfortune, forbearance in prosperity, eloquence in the assembly, valour in battle, eagerness in [seeking] fame, attention to the Vedas—these are natural to a great man.

388. विप्राणां ज्ञानतो ज्यैष्ठ्यं क्षत्रियाणां तु वीर्यतः ।
वैश्यानां धान्यधनतश्शूद्राणामेव जन्मतः ॥

విప్రాణాం జ్ఞానతో జ్యైష్ఠ్యం క్షత్రియాణాం తు వీర్యతః।
వైశ్యానాం ధాన్యధనతశ్శూద్రాణామేవ జన్మతః॥

Among Brahmans, seniority is [attained] by knowledge; among Kshatriyas, by valour; among Vaiśyas, by corn and money; and only among Śûdras, by birth.

(See No. 163.)

389. विभूषणं मौनमपंडितानां ॥

విభూషణం మౌనమపండితానాం॥

Silence is the ornament of the ignorant.

(See No. 169.)

390. विषं सभा दरिद्रस्य वृद्धस्य तरुणी विषं ॥

విషం సభా దరిద్రస్య వృద్ధస్య తరుణీ విషం॥

An assembly is poison to a poor man; a young wife is poison to an old man.

(See TELUGU No. 1779.)

Poor men's words have little weight. (Greek.)*

A young wife is an old man's post-horse to the grave. (German.)†

---

* Τῶν γὰρ πενήτων ἔισιν ὁι λόγοι κένοι.
† Jung Weib ist altem Mann, das Postpferd zum Grabe.

391. **विषकुंभं पयोमुखं ॥**

విషకుంభం పయోముఖం॥

A vessel of poison, with a face of milk.

(See TELUGU No. 4, &c.)

परोक्षे कार्यहंतारं प्रत्यक्षे प्रियवादिनं ।
वर्जयेत्तादृशं मित्रं विषकुंभं पयोमुखं ॥
పరోక్షే కార్యహంతారం ప్రత్యక్షే ప్రియవాదినం।
వర్జయేత్తాదృశం మిత్రం విషకుంభం పయోముఖం॥

Such a friend as, like a vessel of poison with a face (i. e. covering) of milk, ruins [a man's] business behind his back and speaks soft words to his face, must be shunned.

392. **विषक्रिमिन्यायः ॥**

విషక్రిమిన్యాయః॥

Like the worm living in poison.

393. **विषवृक्षोऽपि संवर्ध्य स्वयं छेत्तुमसांप्रतं ॥**

విషవృక్షోఽపి సంవర్ధ్య స్వయం ఛేత్తుమసాంప్రతం॥

It is not right for one to cut down even a poisonous tree which he himself has reared.

इतस्सदैत्यः प्राप्तश्रीर्नेत एवार्हति क्षयं ।
विषवृक्षोऽपि संवर्ध्य स्वयं छेत्तुमसांप्रतं ॥
ఇతస్సదైత్యః ప్రాప్తశ్రీర్నేత ఏవార్హతి క్షయం।
విషవృక్షోఽపి సంవర్ధ్య స్వయం ఛేత్తుమసాంప్రతం॥

Hence has the Daitya derived his prosperity and for this very reason he does not deserve destruction: it is not right for one to cut down even a poisonous tree which he himself has reared.

394. **विषस्य विषमौषधं ॥**

విషస్య విషమౌషధం॥

Poison is the remedy for poison.

दृष्टिं देहि पुनर्बाले हरिणायतलोचने ।
श्रूयते हि पुरा लोके विषस्य विषमौषधं ॥

దృష్టిం దేహి పునర్బాలే హరిణాయతలోచనే।
శ్రూయతే హి పురా లోకే విషస్య విషమౌషధం॥

Caste your sight, broad fawn-eyed damsel, once more [upon me]—have we not heard from the olden time that poison is the remedy for poison?

Poison quells poison. (Italian.)*

One nail drives out another.

395. **विषादप्यमृतं ग्राह्यं बालादपि सुभाषितं ।**
अमित्रादपि सद्वृत्तममेध्यादपि कांचनं ॥

విషాదప్యమృతం గ్రాహ్యం బాలాదపి సుభాషితం।
అమిత్రాదపి సద్వృత్తమమేధ్యాదపి కాంచనం॥

Nectar should be taken even out of poison; a well spoken word should be received even from a youth; rectitude should be acknowledged even in an enemy, and gold should be taken even out of filth.

396. **वृथा वृष्टिस्समुद्रे च वृथा तृप्ते तु भोजनं ।**
वृथा धनपतौ दानं दरिद्रे यौवनं वृथा ॥

వృథా వృష్టిస్సముద్రే చ వృథా తృప్తే తు భోజనం।
వృథా ధనపతౌ దానం దరిద్రే యౌవనం వృథా॥

Useless is rain to the sea, and useless is food to one satisfied; useless is a gift to a rich man, useless is youth to a poor man.

(cf. Böhtlingk's *Indische Sprüche*, 2890, 5031.)

---

* Il veleno si spegne col veleno.

397. वृद्धा नारी पतिव्रता ॥

వృద్ధా నారీ పతివ్రతా॥

An old woman, a chaste wife.

398. वृद्धा वेश्या तपस्विनी ॥

వృద్ధా వేశ్యా తపస్వినీ॥

An old harlot, a female devotee.

अशक्तस्तस्करस्साधुः कुरूपा चेत्पतिव्रता ।
रोगी च देवताभक्तो वृद्धा वेश्या तपस्विनी ॥

అశక్తస్తస్కరస్సాధుః కురూపా చేత్పతివ్రతా।
రోగీ చ దేవతాభక్తో వృద్ధా వేశ్యా తపస్వినీ॥

A feeble thief, a good man; an ugly woman, a chaste wife; a sick man a worshipper of the deity; an old harlot, a female devotee.

399. वृद्धस्य वचनं ग्राह्यमापत्काले ह्युपस्थिते ॥

వృద్ధస్య వచనం గ్రాహ్యమాపత్కాలే హ్యుపస్థితే॥

An old man's advice should be taken in a time of misfortune.

400. वृश्चिकस्य विषं पुच्छं मक्षिकाया विषं शिरः ।
भुजंगस्य विषं दंष्ट्रा सर्वांगं दुर्जने विषं ॥

వృశ్చికస్య విషం పుచ్ఛం మక్షికాయా విషం శిరః।
భుజంగస్య విషం దంష్ట్రా సర్వాంగం దుర్జనే విషం॥

The poison of a scorpion is in his tail; the poison of a fly is in his head; the poison of a serpent is in his fang; the poison of a bad man is in his whole body.

401. वृषभकलहे वत्सपादभंगः ॥

వృషభకలహే వత్సపాదభంగః॥

In a fight between bulls, the calf's leg is broken.

(See TELUGU No. 212.)

402. वैश्यो विश्वासघातकः ॥
వైశ్యో విశ్వాసఘాతకః॥

A Vaiśya is a betrayer of confidence.

403. व्यापारं द्रोहचिंतनं ॥
వ్యాపారం ద్రోహచింతనం॥

Trade is treachery.

An ungrammatical, but common saying, corrupted from "*Vyâpâdo droha chintanam*" in the Amarakośa.

404. व्यासघट्टः ॥
వ్యాసఘట్టః॥

Vyâsa's pass.

Said of "any difficult passage in the Mahâbhârata" or of "any puzzle or stumbling block." (Brown.)

श.

405. शचीपतिर्मघवा वा ॥
శచీపతిర్మఘవా వా॥

Is not Śachipati Maghavâ?

Both names of Indra.

406. शठे शाठ्यं समाचरेत् ॥
శఠే శాఠ్యం సమాచరేత్॥

Deceit must be practised towards the deceitful.

सारल्यं सरले कुर्याच्छठे शाठ्यं समाचरेत् ॥
సారల్యం సరలే కుర్యాచ్ఛఠే శాఠ్యం సమాచరేత్॥

One must be upright towards an upright man and deceitful towards a deceitful man.

407. शतं विहाय भोक्तव्यं ॥

శతం విహాయ భోక్తవ్యం॥

Leave off a hundred [works] and eat.

Food is the first thing.

408. शतश्लोकेन पंडितः ॥

శతశ్లోకేన పండితః॥

A Paṇḍit by a hundred stanzas.

Said derisively.

409. शतेषु जायते शूरस्सहस्रेषु च पंडितः ॥

శతేషు జాయతే శూరస్సహస్రేషు చ పండితః॥

In a hundred, one hero is found; in a thousand, one Paṇḍit.

410. शनैः पंथाः शनैः कंथा ॥

శనైః పంథాః శనైః కంథా॥

Slowly along the road, slowly through the quilt.

A quilt of patch work is referred to.

शनैः पंथाः शनैः कंथा शनैः पर्वतलंघनं ।
शनैः कर्म च धर्मश्च एते पंच शनैः शनैः ॥

శనైః పంథాః శనైః కంథా శనైః పర్వతలంఘనం।
శనైః కర్మ చ ధర్మశ్చ ఏతే పంచ శనైః శనైః॥

Slowly along the road; slowly through the quilt; slowly over the mountain; slowly through your business; slowly in your charities—slowly, slowly, through these five.

The admonition, nothing rashly, is everywhere useful. (Greek.)*

---

* Τὸ μηδὲν εἰκῇ, πανταχοῦ 'στι χρήσιμον.

411. शनैः पर्वतलंघनं ॥

శనైః పర్వతలంఘనం॥

Slowly over the mountain.

अटनेन महारण्ये सुपंथा जायते शनैः ।
वेदाभ्यासात्तथा ज्ञानं शनैः पर्वतलंघनं ॥

అటనేన మహారణ్యే సుపంథా జాయతే శనైః।
వేదాభ్యాసాత్తథా జ్ఞానం శనైః పర్వతలంఘనం॥

The right path will gradually be found in a forest by wandering in it; so wisdom will be gradually acquired by study of the Vedas, as a mountain is slowly crossed.

412. शनैः शनैः क्षिपेत्पादं ॥

శనైః శనైః క్షిపేత్పాదం॥

Slowly, slowly, place the foot.

Be careful in each step you take in any business.

413. शरीरं व्याधिमंदिरं ॥

శరీరం వ్యాధిమందిరం॥

The body is the abode of diseases.

दुःखोपकारसच्चर्याज्ञानं यत्र न भास्वरं ।
वृथा वहति तज्जीवः शरीरं व्याधिमंदिरं ॥

దుఃఖోపకారసచ్చర్యాజ్ఞానం యత్ర న భాస్వరం।
వృథా వహతి తజ్జీవః శరీరం వ్యాధిమందిరం॥

That soul, in which there is no perception of sorrow, beneficence, or virtue [in others], bears in vain a body, the abode of diseases.

414. शरीरमाद्यं खलु धर्मसाधनं ॥
శరీరమాద్యం ఖలు ధర్మసాధనం॥

Is not the body the chief instrument of doing good?

(See No. 261.)

अपि क्रियार्थं सुलभं समित्कुशं जलान्यपि स्नानविधिक्षमाणि ते।
अपि स्वशक्त्या तपसि प्रवर्तसे शरीरमाद्यं खलु धर्मसाधनं ॥
అపి క్రియార్థం సులభం సమిత్కుశం జలాన్యపి స్నానవిధిక్షమాణి తే।
అపి స్వశక్త్యా తపసి ప్రవర్తసే శరీరమాద్యం ఖలు ధర్మసాధనం॥

Are fuel and Kusa grass easy to get? Is the water fit for your bathing? Are you engaged in penance according to your strength? Is not the body the chief instrument of doing good?

Said by Śiva to Pârvatî—(see the Kumâra-sambhava).—*Kuśa* is the Poa cynosuroides.

415. शाकाय वा स्याल्लवणाय वा स्यात् ॥
శాకాయ వా స్యాల్లవణాయ వా స్యాత్॥

It will do for vegetable, or it will do for salt.

Said by a beggar.

416. शापादपि शरादपि ॥
శాపాదపి శరాదపి॥

By curse, and by arrow.

अग्रतश्चतुरो वेदान् पृष्ठतस्सशरं धनुः ।
उभाभ्यां च समर्थोहं शापादपि शरादपि ॥
అగ్రతశ్చతురో వేదాన్ పృష్ఠతస్సశరం ధనుః।
ఉభాభ్యాం చ సమర్థోహం శాపాదపి శరాదపి॥

With the four Vedas before me, and the bow and arrow behind me, I am powerful both by curse and by arrow.

Said by Paraśurâma.

417. शिरो नास्ति शिरोव्यथा ॥

శిరో నాస్తి శిరోవ్యథా॥

No head, but head-ache.

Applied to irrational argument, &c.—(cf. Morton 861.)

418. शीलं सर्वत्र भूषणं ॥

శీలం సర్వత్ర భూషణం॥

Moral rectitude is everywhere an ornament.

i. e., it is an ornament to a man wherever he goes.

419. शुनि दृष्टे न पाषाणः पाषाणे श्वा न दृश्यते ।
दृष्टे शुनि च पाषाणे राजश्वा किं नु कुर्महे ॥

శుని దృష్టే న పాషాణః పాషాణే శ్వా న దృశ్యతే।
దృష్టే శుని చ పాషాణే రాజశ్వా కిం ను కుర్మహే॥

When a dog is seen, there is no stone; when a stone is found, the dog is not seen; when both the dog and stone are seen, then what can we do to the king's dog?

420. शुभस्य शीघ्रं अशुभस्य कालहरणं ॥

శుభస్య శీఘ్రం అశుభస్య కాలహరణం॥

In an auspicious [business] haste, in an inauspicious [business] delay.

421. शुष्कवैरं विवादं च न कुर्यात्केनचित्सह ॥

శుష్కవైరం వివాదం చ న కుర్యాత్కేనచిత్సహ॥

Entertain not groundless enmity towards, nor quarrel with any one.

422. **श्वः कार्यमद्य कर्तव्यं ॥**

శ్వః కార్యమద్య కర్తవ్యం॥

Do to-day what must be done to-morrow.

Be beforehand with your business.

Take time by the forelock.

श्वः कार्यमद्य कर्तव्यं पूर्वाह्णे चापराह्णिकं ।
न हि प्रतीक्षते मृत्युः कृतमस्य न वा कृतं ॥

శ్వః కార్యమద్య కర్తవ్యం పూర్వాహ్ణే చాపరాహ్ణికం।
న హి ప్రతీక్షతే మృత్యుః కృతమస్య న వా కృతం॥

The business of to-morrow should be done to-day, and that of the after-noon in the forenoon : Death waits not, whether the thing be done or not done.

423. **श्वशुरगृहं परमसुखं त्रिरात्राच्छुनकसमानः ॥**

శ్వశురగృహం పరమసుఖం త్రిరాత్రాచ్ఛునకసమానః॥

In the father-in-law's house is the greatest happiness, but after the third night [the son-in-law is treated] like a dog.

424. **श्वानारोहे कुतस्सौख्यं ॥**

శ్వానారోహే కుతస్సౌఖ్యం॥

Where is the pleasure in mounting a dog ?

ष .

425. **षट्कर्णो भिद्यते मंत्रः ॥**

షట్కర్ణో భిద్యతే మంత్రః॥

The six-eared counsel is split.

i. e., nothing remains secret which is known to three persons.

षट्कर्णो भिद्यते मंत्रस्तथा प्राप्तश्च वार्तया ।
इतिमंत्रिद्वितीयेन मंत्रः कार्यो महीभुजा ॥

షట్కర్ణో భిద్యతే మంత్రస్తథా ప్రాప్తశ్చ వార్తయా।
ఇతిమంత్రిద్వితీయేన మంత్రః కార్యో మహీభుజా॥

[Knowing] that counsel is divulged by six ears and spread by report, a king should take counsel [only] with a second, his minister.

(cf. Hitopadesa, Book III.)

426. षड्भिः कर्णो निपातितः ॥

షడ్భిః కర్ణో నిపాతితః॥

By six, was Karṇa made to fall.

त्वया मया च कुंत्या च धरण्या वासवेन च ।
जामदग्न्येन रामेण षड्भिः कर्णो निपातितः ॥
త్వయా మయా చ కుంత్యా చ ధరణ్యా వాసవేన చ।
జామదగ్న్యేన రామేణ షడ్భిః కర్ణో నిపాతితః॥

By you, by me, by Kuntî, by the Earth, by Vâsava, and by Râma, the son of Jamadagni—by six was Karṇa ruined.

427. षण्णां रसानां लवणं प्रधानं ॥

షణ్ణాం రసానాం లవణం ప్రధానం॥

Of the six flavours, salt is the chief.

The others are sweet, pungent, bitter, sour, and astringent.

स.

428. संतस्स्वयं परहिते विहिताभियोगाः ॥

సంతస్స్వయం పరహితే విహితాభియోగాః॥

Good men are energetic in seeking the good of others.

429. संतोषो नंदने वने ॥

సంతోషో నందనే వనే॥

Happiness is in the Nandana garden.

Nandana is Indra's pleasure ground.

430. संप्रीतिभोज्यान्यन्नानि ॥

సంప్రీతిభోజ్యాన్యన్నాని॥

Food should be eaten with affection.

(See TELUGU No. 1581, &c.)

431. संसर्गजा दोषगुणा भवंति ॥

సంసర్గజా దోషగుణా భవంతి॥

Vice and virtue spring from association.

माताप्येका पिताप्येको मम तस्य च पक्षिणः ।
अहं मुनिभिरानीतस्स चानीतो गवाशनैः ॥
अहं मुनीनां वचनं शृणोमि गवाशनानां स वचश्शृणोति ।
न तस्य दोषा न गुणा ममापि संसर्गजा दोषगुणा भवंति॥

మాతాప్యేకా పితాప్యేకో మమ తస్య చ పక్షిణః।
అహం మునిభిరానీతస్స చానీతో గవాశనైః॥
అహం మునీనాం వచనం శృణోమి గవాశనానాం స వచశ్శృణోతి।
న తస్య దోషా న గుణా మమాపి సంసర్గజా దోషగుణా భవంతి॥

The mother and the father of me and of that bird are one; I was brought by Munis and he was taken by Gavâśanas; I hear the Munis' speech and he hears that of the Gavâśanas; neither are his defects nor are mine good qualities—vice and virtue spring from association.

Gavâśanas [*lit.* "beef-eaters"] are outcastes.

432. संसारसागरे दुःखं ॥

సంసారసాగరే దుఃఖం॥

In the world's ocean is grief.

433. संसारी दुःखी, सन्न्यासी सुखी ॥

సంసారీ దుఃఖీ సన్న్యాసీ సుఖీ॥

The worldly man is a man of sorrows, the Sannyâsî is a man of joys.

434. सकलं शीलेन कुर्याद्वशं ॥
సకలం శీలేన కుర్యాద్వశం॥

A good disposition gains all.

मित्रं स्वच्छतया रिपुं नयबलैर्लुब्धं धनैरीश्वरं
कार्येण द्विजमादरेण युवतिं प्रेम्णा शमैर्बांधवान् ।
अत्युग्रंस्तुतिभिर्गुरुं प्रणतिभिर्मूर्खं कथाभिर्बुधं
विद्याभीरसिकं रसेन सकलं शीलेन कुर्याद्वशं ॥

మిత్రం స్వచ్ఛతయా రిపుం నయబలైర్లుబ్ధం ధనైరీశ్వరం
కార్యేణ ద్విజమాదరేణ యువతిం ప్రేమ్ణా శమైర్బాంధవాన్।
అత్యుగ్రంస్తుతిభిర్గురుం ప్రణతిభిర్మూర్ఖం కథాభిర్బుధం
విద్యాభీరసికం రసేన సకలం శీలేన కుర్యాద్వశం॥

A friend can be gained by transparency [of conduct]; an enemy, by prudence and power; a miser, by money; a master, by service; a brahman, by kindness; a young wife, by tenderness; relatives, by patience; a passionate man, by praise; a priest, by reverence; a fool, by stories; a wise man, by learning; a man with a taste, by humouring him; and all, by good conduct.

435. सति कुड्ये चित्रकर्म ॥
సతి కుడ్యే చిత్రకర్మ॥

Where there's a wall, you can draw on it.

(See TELUGU No. 824.)

436. सत्पुत्रः कुलदीपकः ॥
సత్పుత్రః కులదీపకః॥

A good son is the light of his family.

शर्वरीदीपकश्चंद्रः प्रभाते दीपको रविः ।
त्रैलोक्यदीपको धर्मस्सत्पुत्रः कुलदीपकः ॥
శర్వరీదీపకశ్చంద్రః ప్రభాతే దీపకో రవిః।
త్రైలోక్యదీపకో ధర్మస్సత్పుత్రః కులదీపకః॥

The moon is the light of the night, the sun is the light of the day; virtue is the light of the three worlds; a good son is the light of his family.

(cf. Böhtlingk's *Indische Sprüche* 2968.)

437. सत्यं ब्रूयात्प्रियं ब्रूयान्न ब्रूयात्सत्यमप्रियं ।
प्रियं च नानृतं ब्रूयादेष धर्मस्सनातनः ॥
సత్యం బ్రూయాత్ప్రియం బ్రూయాన్న బ్రూయాత్సత్యమప్రియం।
ప్రియం చ నానృతం బ్రూయాదేష ధర్మస్సనాతనః॥

Speak the truth, and speak to please; speak not the truth, to displease; speak not untruth, to please; this is eternal virtue.

438. सत्येन लोकान्जयति ॥
సత్యేన లోకాన్జయతి॥

By truth, he conquers the worlds.

439. सत्रे भुक्तिर्मठे निद्रा ॥
సత్రే భుక్తిర్మఠే నిద్రా॥

Eating in a Satram, sleeping in a Maṭha.

Satram (Chuttrum) is a travellers' rest-house ; *Maṭha* is a convent.

Said of one who leads a wandering life.

440. सत्संगतिः कथय किं न करोति पुंसां ॥
సత్సంగతిః కథయ కిం న కరోతి పుంసాం॥

Say, what does not good association do for men?

जाड्यं धियो हरति सिंचति वाचि सत्यं ।
मानोन्नतिं दिशति पापमपाकरोति ॥
चेतः प्रसादयति दिक्षु तनोति कीर्तिं ।
सत्संगतिः कथय किं न करोति पुंसां ॥
జాడ్యం ధియో హరతి సించతి వాచి సత్యం।
మానోన్నతిం దిశతి పాపమపాకరోతి॥
చేతః ప్రసాదయతి దిక్షు తనోతి కీర్తిం।
సత్సంగతిః కథయ కిం న కరోతి పుంసాం॥

Say, what does not good association do for men? It removes the dulness of their intellects ; it sprinkles truth in their speech ; it gains the highest honors for them ; expels sin from them ; it purifies their mind ; and spreads their fame towards all quarters.

441. सद्यः फलं तु संगीतं ॥

సద్యః ఫలం తు సంగీతం॥

The effect of music is immediate.

442. सद्यो ददातिचतुरः सद्यो नास्तीति चतुरतमः ॥

సద్యో దదాతిచతురః సద్యో నాస్తీతి చతురతమః॥

A wise man gives at once, a wiser man at once refuses.

443. सद्विद्या यदि किं धनैरपयशो यद्यस्ति किं मृत्युना ॥

సద్విద్యా యది కిం ధనైరపయశో యద్యస్తి కిం మృత్యునా॥

If there be great learning, what of money? If there be an ill name, what of death?

444. स बंधुर्यो हितेषु स्यात् स पिता यस्तु पोषकः ।
स सखा यत्र विश्वासस्सा भार्या यत्र निर्वृतिः ॥

స బంధుర్యో హితేషు స్యాత్ స పితా యస్తు పోషకః।
స సఖా యత్ర విశ్వాసస్సా భార్యా యత్ర నిర్వృతిః॥

Who befriends, he is a relation; who supports, he is a father; he is a friend, in whom there is confidence; she is a wife, in whom there is pleasure.

445. सभा वा न प्रवेष्टव्या वक्तव्यं वा समंजसं ।
अब्रुवन्विब्रुवन्वापि नरो भवति किल्बिषी ॥

సభా వా న ప్రవేష్టవ్యా వక్తవ్యం వా సమంజసం।
అబ్రువన్విబ్రువన్వాపి నరో భవతి కిల్బిషీ॥

Either go not into an assembly, or if you go, speak well; if a man speak not, or speak badly, he becomes a sinner.

446. समाश्रयबलादेव गरुडं यांतमध्वनि ।

पिनाकपाणिपाणिस्थः कुशलं पृष्टवानहिः ॥

సమాశ్రయబలాదేవ గరుడం యాంతమధ్వని।

పినాకపాణిపాణిస్థః కుశలం పృష్టవానహిః॥

On the strength of his position, the serpent dwelling on the wrist of Pinâkapâṇi (Śiva) asked Garuḍa when going along the road, whether he was well.

(See TELUGU No. 751.)

447. सर्वं परवशं दुःखं सर्वमात्मवशं सुखं ॥

సర్వం పరవశం దుఃఖం సర్వమాత్మవశం సుఖం॥

All entrusted to another is grief, all undertaken by one's self is joy.

यद्यत्परवशं कर्म तत्तद्यत्नेन वर्जयेत् ।
यद्यदात्मवशं तु स्यात्तत्तत्सेवेत यत्नतः ॥
सर्वं परवशं दुःखं सर्वमात्मवशं सुखं ।
एतद्विद्यात्समासेन लक्षणं सुखदुःखयोः ॥

యద్యత్పరవశం కర్మ తత్తద్యత్నేన వర్జయేత్।
యద్యదాత్మవశం తు స్యాత్తత్తత్సేవేత యత్నతః॥
సర్వం పరవశం దుఃఖం సర్వమాత్మవశం సుఖం।
ఏతద్విద్యాత్సమాసేన లక్షణం సుఖదుఃఖయోః॥

Endeavour should be made to relinquish whatever business is in another's hands; that which is in one's own hands should be done earnestly: all entrusted to another is grief; all undertaken by one's self is joy; these should be known, in short, as the characteristics of joy and sorrow.

Self do, self have.

If you would have a thing well done, do it yourself.

The master orders the man, the man orders the cat, and the cat orders her tail. (Portuguese.)*

* Manda o amo ao moço, o moço ao gato, e o gato ao rabo.

448. सर्वमेकं जगन्नाथे ॥
సర్వమేకం జగన్నాథే॥

At Jagannâtha, all are one.

No caste distinctions in eating.

449. सर्वस्य गात्रस्य शिरः प्रधानं ॥
సర్వస్య గాత్రస్య శిరః ప్రధానం॥

In the whole body, the head is chief.

450. सर्वस्स्वार्थं समीहते ॥
సర్వస్స్వార్థం సమీహతే॥

All seek their own object

यजतां पांडवस्स्वर्गमवत्विंद्रस्तपत्विनः ।
वयं हनाम द्विषतस्सर्वस्स्वार्थं समीहते ॥
యజతాం పాండవస్స్వర్గమవత్వింద్రస్తపత్వినః।
వయం హనామ ద్విషతస్సర్వస్స్వార్థం సమీహతే॥

Let the Pâṇḍava sacrifice; let Indra protect Svarga; let the sun shine; we will kill our enemies—all seek their own object.

451. सर्वैरुपायैः फलमेव साध्यं ॥
సర్వైరుపాయైః ఫలమేవ సాధ్యం॥

By every means, one's object must be accomplished.

त्रिविक्रमोभूदपि वामनोसौ स सूकरश्चेति स वै नृसिंहः ।
नीचैरनीचैरतिनीचनीचैस्सर्वैरुपायैः फलमेव साध्यं ॥
త్రివిక్రమోభూదపి వామనోసౌ స సూకరశ్చేతి స వై నృసింహః।
నీచైరనీచైరతినీచనీచైస్సర్వైరుపాయైః ఫలమేవ సాధ్యం॥

Though a dwarf, he (Vishṇu) became Trivikrama and Sûkara and Nṛisiṁha; by all means, whether base or not base, or the basest of the base, one's object must be accomplished.

452. सर्वेंद्रियाणां नयनं प्रधानं ॥
సర్వేంద్రియాణాం నయనం ప్రధానం॥
Of all the senses, sight is the chief.

453. सर्वे जना: कांचनमाश्रयंति ॥
సర్వే జనాః కాంచనమాశ్రయంతి॥
All people seek gold.

(See No. 345.)

454. सर्वे जनास्सुखिनो भवंतु ॥
సర్వే జనాస్సుఖినో భవంతు॥
May all people be happy!
Said on auspicious occasions.

455. सहवासत: पुण्यगुणा भवंति सहवासतो दोषगुणा भवंति ॥
సహవాసతః పుణ్యగుణా భవంతి సహవాసతో దోషగుణా భవంతి॥
By association good qualities are acquired, by association bad qualities are acquired.

(See No. 431.)

456. सहसा विदधीत न क्रियां ॥
సహసా విదధీత న క్రియాం॥
No business should be done rashly.

(See No. 410.)

457. सहायो बलवत्तर: ॥
సహాయో బలవత్తరః॥
A companion is an additional strength.

(See TELUGU No. 480.)

सगुणो निर्गुणो वापि सहायो बलवत्तर: ।
तुषेणापि परिभ्रष्टस्तंडुलो नांकुरायते ॥
సగుణో నిర్గుణో వాపి సహాయో బలవత్తరః।
తుషేణాపి పరిభ్రష్టస్తండులో నాంకురాయతే॥

Whether he have talent or be without it, a companion is an additional strength; if deprived of husk the rice will not sprout.

458. **साहसाद्भजते लक्ष्मीः ॥**
సాహసాద్భజతే లక్ష్మీః॥

Fortune is secured by boldness.

Fortune favors the bold. (Latin.)*

459. **साहसे लक्ष्मीः ॥**
సాహసే లక్ష్మీః॥

Fortune is in boldness.

460. **सिकतालवालं ॥**
సికతాలవాలం॥

A flower-bed of sand.

461. **सिद्धमन्नं परित्यज्य भिक्षामटति दुर्मतिः ॥**
సిద్ధమన్నం పరిత్యజ్య భిక్షామటతి దుర్మతిః॥

A foolish man leaves the food which is ready for him and goes to beg.

462. **सुखस्यानंतरं दुःखं दुःखस्यानंतरं सुखं ।**
चक्रवत्परिवर्तंते दुःखानि च सुखानि च ॥
సుఖస్యానంతరం దుఃఖం దుఃఖస్యానంతరం సుఖం।
చక్రవత్పరివర్తంతే దుఃఖాని చ సుఖాని చ॥

After happiness, sorrow; after sorrow, happiness; happiness and sorrow revolve like a discus.

(See TELUGU Nos. 561, 568.)

Joy and sorrow are next-door neighbours. (German.)†

463. **सूचीकटाहन्यायः ॥**
సూచీకటాహన్యాయః॥

A needle and a boiler.

The first takes a short time to make, it should therefore be made first.

---

* Fortes fortuna adjuvat.
† Freud' und Leid sind nahe Nachbarn.

464. **सेवकान्नं पुरातनं ॥**

సేవకాన్నం పురాతనం॥

A servant and food [are good] old.

नवं वस्त्रं नवं छत्रं नव्या स्त्री नूतनं गृहं ।
सर्वत्र नूतनं शस्तं सेवकान्नं पुरातनं ॥

నవం వస్త్రం నవం ఛత్రం నవ్యా స్త్రీ నూతనం గృహం।
సర్వత్ర నూతనం శస్తం సేవకాన్నం పురాతనం॥

A new cloth, a new umbrella, a new wife, a new house are everywhere good new ; a servant and food are good old.

465. **स्यालको गृहनाशाय सर्वनाशाय मातुलः ॥**

స్యాలకో గృహనాశాయ సర్వనాశాయ మాతులః॥

A brother-in-law is the ruin of the house, a maternal uncle is the ruin of everything.

466. **स्त्रियाश्चरित्रं पुरुषस्य भाग्यं देवा न जानंति कुतो मनुष्याः ॥**

స్త్రియాశ్చరిత్రం పురుషస్య భాగ్యం దేవా న జానంతి కుతో మనుష్యాః॥

The gods know not a woman's conduct and a man's fortune, how then can men?

467. **स्त्रियो मूलमनर्थानां ॥**

స్త్రియో మూలమనర్థానాం॥

Women are the cause of mischief.

468. **स्त्रीणां द्विगुण आहारो बुद्धिश्चापि चतुर्गुणा ।**
साहसं षड्गुणं चैव कामोष्टगुण उच्यते ॥

స్త్రీణాం ద్విగుణ ఆహారో బుద్ధిశ్చాపి చతుర్గుణా।
సాహసం షడ్గుణం చైవ కామోష్టగుణ ఉచ్యతే॥

Women are said to eat twice as much [as men], to have four times as much sense, six times as much pluck, and eight times as much desire.

(Cf. Böhtlingk's *Indische Sprüche* 412, 5306.)

469. **स्त्रीणामालोचनं विना ॥**

స్త్రీణామాలోచనం వినా॥

Without the advice of women.

i. e. Admit not women into your counsels.

470. **स्त्रीरत्नं दुष्कुलादपि ॥**

స్త్రీరత్నం దుష్కులాదపి॥

Take an excellent woman even from a bad caste.

श्रद्दधानः शुभां विद्यामाददीतावरादपि ।
अंत्यादपि परं धर्मं स्त्रीरत्नं दुष्कुलादपि ॥

శ్రద్దధానః శుభాం విద్యామాదదీతావరాదపి।
అంత్యాదపి పరం ధర్మం స్త్రీరత్నం దుష్కులాదపి॥

An assiduous man should receive good learning even from a low fellow; excellent virtue even from an outcaste, and an excellent woman [*lit.* a woman-gem] even from a bad caste.

471. **स्थानस्थितः कापुरुषोपि सिंहः ॥**

స్థానస్థితః కాపురుషోపి సింహః॥

In a strong position, even a coward is a lion.

(See TELUGU No. 2124.)

जानामि रे सर्प तव प्रभावं कंठस्थितो गर्जसि शंकरस्य ।
स्थानं प्रधानं न बलं प्रधानं स्थानस्थितः कापुरुषोपि सिंहः ॥

జానామి రే సర్ప తవ ప్రభావం కంఠస్థితో గర్జసి శంకరస్య।
స్థానం ప్రధానం న బలం ప్రధానం స్థానస్థితః కాపురుషోపి సింహః॥

O Serpent! I know thy power; dwelling on the neck of Śankara (Śiva), thou dost hiss : position is the chief thing, not strength ;—even a coward is a lion in a strong position.

472. स्थालीपुलाकन्यायः ॥

స్థాలీపులాకన్యాయః॥

The pot and a grain of boiled rice.

(See TELUGU No. 1921.)

473. स्थितस्य गतिश्चिंतनीया ॥

స్థితస్య గతిశ్చింతనీయా॥

The disposal of what remains should be thought of.

Without vain regrets for what has gone.

474. स्नेहे च बंधुर्न कदापि दूरः ॥

స్నేహే చ బంధుర్న కదాపి దూరః॥

Where there is friendship, the friend is never far off.

(See TELUGU No. 186.)

475. स्वकार्यधुरंधरास्स्वामिकार्यवंचकाः ॥

స్వకార్యధురంధరాస్స్వామికార్యవంచకాః॥

Hard working men in their own business, but rogues in their master's business.

(See TELUGU No. 2652.)

476. स्वकार्यमुद्धरेत्प्राज्ञः कार्यध्वंसे च मूर्खता ॥

స్వకార్యముద్ధరేత్ప్రాజ్ఞః కార్యధ్వంసే చ మూర్ఖతా॥

A wise man gains his object; in failure is foolishness.

अवमानं पुरस्कृत्य मानं कृत्वा च पृष्ठतः ।
स्वकार्यमुद्धरेत्प्राज्ञः कार्यध्वंसे च मूर्खता ॥
అవమానం పురస్కృత్య మానం కృత్వా చ పృష్ఠతః।
స్వకార్యముద్ధరేత్ప్రాజ్ఞః కార్యధ్వంసే చ మూర్ఖతా॥

Disregarding honor and even courting dishonor, a wise man gains his object; in failure is foolishness.

477. स्वगृहे को विचारोस्ति ॥

స్వగృహే కో విచారోస్తి॥

What deliberation is there in one's own house?

Said by very intimate friends, meaning that no formality is required to be observed by them in each other's houses.

478. स्वगृहे पूज्यते मूर्खः स्वग्रामे पूज्यते प्रभुः ।
स्वदेशे पूज्यते राजा विद्वान्सर्वत्र पूज्यते ॥

స్వగృహే పూజ్యతే మూర్ఖః స్వగ్రామే పూజ్యతే ప్రభుః।
స్వదేశే పూజ్యతే రాజా విద్వాన్సర్వత్ర పూజ్యతే॥

A fool is honored in his own house; a proprietor is honored in his own village; a king is honored in his own country; a learned man is honored everywhere.

479. स्वभावो मूर्ध्नि वर्तते ॥

స్వభావో మూర్ధ్ని వర్తతే॥

The natural disposition stands at the head.

सर्वस्य हि परीक्ष्यंते स्वभावा नेतरे गुणाः ।
अतीत्य हि गुणान् सर्वान्स्वभावो मूर्ध्नि वर्तते ॥

సర్వస్య హి పరీక్ష్యంతే స్వభావా నేతరే గుణాః।
అతీత్య హి గుణాన్ సర్వాన్స్వభావో మూర్ధ్ని వర్తతే॥

The natural disposition of every one is investigated, not the other qualities; the natural disposition excelling all other qualities, stands at the head of them.

480. स्वयं तीर्त्वा परान् तारयेत् ॥

స్వయం తీర్త్వా పరాన్ తారయేత్॥

Having crossed yourself, get others across.

Help yourself first and then others.

Self's the man. (Dutch.)*

---

* Zelf is de Man.

481. स्वानुष्ठानस्य समये मुनयोपि न पंडिताः ॥

స్వానుష్ఠానస్య సమయే మునయోపి న పండితాః॥

In their own actions even Munis are not wise.

परोपदेशसमये सर्वं एव हि पंडिताः ।
स्वानुष्ठानस्य समये मुनयोपि न पंडिताः ॥
పరోపదేశసమయే సర్వ ఏవ హి పండితాః।
స్వానుష్ఠానస్య సమయే మునయోపి న పండితాః॥

In teaching others, all are wise; but in their own actions even Munis are not w

ह.

482. हलांतं ब्रह्मवर्चसं ॥

హలాంతం బ్రహ్మవర్చసం॥

Sanctity as far as the plough.

If a Brahman commence to till the ground, he loses his sanctity.

483. हसद्भिः क्रियते कर्म रुदद्भिरनुभूयते ॥

హసద్భిః క్రియతే కర్మ రుదద్భిరనుభూయతే॥

Laughing, a thing is done; weeping, the fruit of it is suffere

(See TELUGU No. 2425.)

484. हस्तिमशकांतरं ॥

హస్తిమశకాంతరం॥

The difference between an elephant and a muskito.

क्ष.

485. क्षणं वित्तं क्षणं चित्तं क्षणं जीवितमावयोः ॥

క్షణం విత్తం క్షణం చిత్తం క్షణం జీవితమావయోః॥

Wealth for a moment, the mind for a moment, our life for a moment

क्षणं वित्तं क्षणं चित्तं क्षणं जीवितमावयोः ।
यमस्य करुणा नास्ति धर्मस्य त्वरिता गतिः ॥
క్షణం విత్తం క్షణం చిత్తం క్షణం జీవితమావయోః।
యమస్య కరుణా నాస్తి ధర్మస్య త్వరితా గతిః॥

Wealth for a moment, mind for a moment, our life for a moment; Yama has no pity, [therefore] do good works quickly.

(See No. 24.)

486. क्षीणे कस्यास्ति गौरवं ॥
క్షీణే కస్యాస్తి గౌరవం॥

Who is honored in adversity?

वनानि दहते वह्निस्सखा भवति मारुतः ।
स एव दीपनाशाय क्षीणे कस्यास्ति गौरवं ॥
వనాని దహతే వహ్నిస్సఖా భవతి మారుతః।
స ఏవ దీపనాశాయ క్షీణే కస్యాస్తి గౌరవం॥

Fire burns forests and Wind is a friend [assists]; but that very Wind proves destructive to the lamp. Who is honored when reduced [in circumstances?]

487. क्षीणे पुण्ये मर्त्यलोकं विशंति ॥
క్షీణే పుణ్యే మర్త్యలోకం విశంతి॥

When the reward of good deeds is ended, [souls] come back to the world of men.

488. क्षीरोदकन्यायः ॥
క్షీరోదకన్యాయః॥

Like milk and water.

(See TELUGU No. 1283, &c.)

Close friendship.